LIFE'S TOO SHORT TO GO
SO F*CKING SLOW

LIFE'S TOO SHORT TO GO SO F*CKING SLOW

LESSONS FROM AN EPIC FRIENDSHIP THAT WENT THE DISTANCE

SUSAN LACKE

VELO press

BOULDER, COLORADO

velopress®

3002 Sterling Circle, Suite 100
Boulder, CO 80301–2338 USA

VeloPress is the leading publisher of books on endurance sports. Focused on cycling, triathlon, running, swimming, and nutrition/diet, VeloPress books help athletes achieve their goals of going faster and farther. Preview books and contact us at velopress.com.

Distributed in the United States and Canada by Ingram Publisher Services

A Cataloging-in-Publication record for this book is available from the Library of Congress.
ISBN 978-1-937715-65-6

This paper meets the requirements of ANSI/NISO Z39.48-1992 (Permanence of Paper).

Art direction by Vicki Hopewell
Cover design by Jonathan Sainsbury
Interior design by Jack Lenzo
Photos: front cover, Getty Images; p. 161, Alex Manville;
p. 167, Aliza Rae Photography; back cover, courtesy of Susan Lacke

17 18 19 / 10 9 8 7 6 5 4 3 2 1

For Carlos

CONTENTS

INTRODUCTION

RUNNING IS FOR CRAZY PEOPLE

"Running is for crazy people." I stubbed out my cigarette and continued ranting to myself. "There's no reason to run unless someone is chasing you. *Those* people are like a cult. They're brainwashed into being completely absorbed by this lifestyle. They even get tattoos after doing a race to declare they were initiated into that stupid cult! It's ridiculous."

Never mind that *those people* were my friends. Sure, I loved them, but let's be clear—I loved them *despite* the fact that they were always exercising and doing triathlons and eating weird foods. I just didn't get it, any of it. And though I knew they weren't trying to talk with an air of superiority, when they shared how they'd just gotten back from a 2-hour bike ride or a 10-mile run, I still somehow felt judged, the outsider who preferred happy hour to spin class.

Ten miles? At 23 years old, tired, stressed, and overweight, I couldn't fathom walking *one* mile, much less running 10.

I knew my unhealthy habits were wrong, but I found ways to justify them.

Smoking caused lung cancer, yes, but it alleviated my stress. That made it all right in my book.

Alcohol? My rational mind knew I wasn't going to find answers to life's problems at the bottom of a bottle, yet at the end of every stressful workday, I poured myself a drink to unwind. And another one to help me forget the day. Then another to help me sleep.

As for exercise, I certainly didn't have time for that. As a first-year college professor with a demanding boss, I had too much work to do.

And although I frequented fast-food chains (who had time to cook?), at least I usually chose a salad (with extra ranch dressing). Sure, a Big Gulp of Diet Dr. Pepper was my constant companion, but that was because I needed the caffeine to keep me going and the carbonation to quell the nausea from last night's tequila.

I had gained 40 pounds in the span of a year. My marriage of four months was beginning to unravel at the seams, as was I. I questioned whether the decision to move from

Wisconsin to Arizona to take my first teaching job had been the right one. It was too much change, too much pressure, and I felt unprepared to handle it.

One day, I was smoking outside my office when my boss came up to me and pointed at the cigarette in my hand. "Mind if I have a drag?" he queried.

I was shocked. Aside from a curt "Welcome" on my first day on campus, Dr. Nunez had never spoken directly to me. I was perfectly fine with that. I found everything about him intimidating, from the way he leaned back in his chair to stare at people while they were talking to his daily disappearances at lunchtime to swim laps in the campus pool. As an engineering professor, he had a bias toward technical and analytical brains that he did not try to hide. When he had been assigned to oversee some majors within the social sciences, which included mine, his irritation had been unmistakable: "Why?" he'd lamented. "It's not even a *real* science." Physically, he was a regimented, imposing figure with long limbs and muscled arms, which he liked to cross over his chest. I was convinced that he had been placed on this earth to intimidate the hell out of me. I did everything I could to avoid crossing his path.

Yet there he was, sitting in a cloud of my Marlboro Light smoke with outstretched fingers.

"Well?" Dr. Nunez smiled. *Dr. Nunez knew how to smile?* Shocked, I handed him my cigarette and watched as he took it between his fingers and stared expectantly at the wisp of smoke curling up from around his knees. He lifted the cigarette, smiled at me once more, and stubbed it out in the nearby ashtray.

"You don't need that shit." He stood up and extended his hand. "Come on, let's go get some coffee."

I was infuriated. *That was my last smoke!* I wanted to yell. Instead, I sat dumbfounded in the shade cast by Dr. Nunez's broad shoulders, too stunned by his bold gesture to say anything.

"I *said*," Dr. Nunez sighed with obvious irritation, "let's go get some coffee."

I quickly scrambled to my feet. "Umm . . . okay?"

Over Americanos, Dr. Nunez asked a lot of questions—*Why do you smoke? If smoking makes you less stressed, what's making you so stressed in the first place?* He listened to my answers intently, interjecting an occasional nod and a "Hmm." His demeanor was disarming, and I felt it drawing me in. Despite knowing better, I found myself committing the incredibly unprofessional crime of unloading all my personal problems on my boss. During a pause in the conversation, I felt a sudden wave of regret—what was I thinking, spilling all this, and to Dr. Nunez of all people? But to my surprise, he didn't lecture me. Instead, he tipped his head thoughtfully, pursed his lips, and said matter-of-factly: "You should come swimming with me during lunch tomorrow."

I laughed out loud. I couldn't help it. "Listen, sir," I said once I'd composed myself, "that's very nice, but I'm not one of those people."

"'Those people'?"

"Crazy people. Health nuts," I blurted out before realizing I had most likely offended the man who signed my paycheck.

"C'mon!" he scoffed. "Swimming is fun! But don't take my word for it. You should try it for yourself." When I hesitated, he added, "If nothing else, you'll get a good suntan out of it."

Did I mention that sunbathing was one of my vices, too?

The next day, as planned, Dr. Nunez showed up at my office door at 11:45 on the dot. Slung over his shoulder was a bag of kickboards and swim paddles.

"You ready?"

I nodded meekly, hoping I was feigning enthusiasm convincingly. He smiled and nodded toward the exit.

"Let's go."

I went swimming that day. And the next. And the next. At first it was out of fear of offending my boss, but soon I found myself starting to look forward to it. I wasn't fast, but I was capable, and I liked spending an hour each day in the Arizona sunshine.

In between laps, Dr. Nunez became Carlos, and Carlos became my friend. It didn't make sense—an athletic, accomplished guy like him had no reason to take an interest in a slow, chubby kid who made poor choices. Still, I decided not to question it.

Over the span of our 10-year friendship, my unhealthy vices disappeared one by one. Cigarettes were eventually replaced with running. Stress was hammered out on the pedals of a bike. And Big Gulps of Diet Dr. Pepper and tequila were replaced with post-ride Americanos with my new mentor.

I didn't realize it at the time, but that Marlboro Light break outside my office building essentially upended my life, changing it forever.

I could easily tell you, in boring detail and with tedious data sets, all about how I became one of *those* people I had long derided. I could tell you what workouts I did to set a personal best time in the marathon or finish my first Ironman®. I could suggest what you should eat or drink or wear. But that's not the real story. Running and triathlon didn't transform me. My friendship with Carlos Nunez—cemented in 100-degree trail runs and Sunday-morning bike rides—did.

1 |

OH MY GOD, I'M FRIENDS WITH A CRAZY PERSON

On paper, our friendship didn't make a lot of sense.

Carlos was a Mexican immigrant who had worked his way out of poverty to achieve the American dream. I was a white kid from the Midwest who took that American dream for granted.

He was an imposing figure, with broad shoulders, a trim waist, a shaved head, and a confident swagger. I was 40 pounds overweight and forgot to comb my hair most mornings.

He taught engineering; I taught human development. He was 42; I was 23. He had his shit together; I most assuredly did not.

Really, there was no reason for the two of us to ever interact beyond his responsibilities as my boss. As the chair of the Technology and Consumer Sciences Department of our college, he only needed to conduct my teaching evaluation once a year.

And yet every day, he would appear in the doorway of my office, duffel bag in hand.

"Let's go." It wasn't a request.

We'd walk across the campus together, my short shuffle rushing to keep up with his long strides.

"How are you?" he'd ask.

"I'm good," I'd say.

"Yeah?"

"Yeah."

And then he'd wait, intentionally creating pockets of silence in the conversation, which drove me crazy. I would panic in the quiet, looking for something—anything—to fill the void. I'd blather on about a lecture that hadn't gone well, rehash a discussion I'd had with a colleague, or share that I hadn't slept well the night before. If all else failed, the weather was my go-to—anything to avoid another second of uncomfortable silence.

It was a relief when we crossed paths with a colleague or student. Where most people simply exchanged hellos in passing, Carlos would stop, greet the person by name, and ask, "How are you?" Then he'd wait patiently for the answer.

The more time I spent with Carlos, the more I realized that my initial perception of him—a cold, intimidating, silent figure—had been dead wrong. I had been cowering in my office, trying to avoid crossing his path, and everyone else on campus seemed to go out of their way to place themselves in it. A half-mile walk across campus sometimes took 20 or 30 minutes.

I didn't understand it. Carlos didn't have a particularly effusive personality. His expression usually remained the same whether his conversation partners were sharing news of a promotion, a death in the family, or the pastrami sandwich they'd had for lunch. Furthermore, he never, ever disclosed anything about himself in return.

I was spending an hour of my day, every day, with someone I knew nothing about. When it came to communication, I was an open book and he was Fort Knox. It drove me absolutely crazy. So one day I decided to give him a taste of his own medicine.

"Hey," I barked as I knocked on his office door one day. "How are you?"

He looked up from his computer with a puzzled expression. Normally, he was the one standing in my office door. The new dynamic concerned him. "Are you okay?"

"Yes, I'm great." I sat down across the desk from him, leaning back in the chair with my arms folded. "How about you? *How are you?*"

Carlos laughed uncomfortably. "Are you sure you're okay?"

"Yeah."

"Yeah?"

We sat there in silence, Carlos meeting my aggressively uncomfortable eye contact with a baffled stare. I was going to wait him out.

Twenty seconds passed. I was going to win this battle.

A minute. I would push down my discomfort, embrace the silence, and . . .

"Gah!" I finally snapped, unable to stand the quiet any longer. "I don't understand! How do you just sit there without talking?"

Carlos leaned back in his chair, clearly amused to have won a battle of wills he didn't even know he had entered. His aloofness was grating to my psyche.

"You know what's sad?" I said impulsively. "You're the closest thing I have to a friend here in Arizona." It was the truth. My friends were 2,000 miles away in Wisconsin. Since the move to Arizona, my work hadn't left me with much time to socialize, aside from the hour I spent quietly swimming in the lane next to my boss.

Carlos cocked his head, not sure what to make of this. "Uh . . . thank you?"

"And I know nothing about you. Nothing. You ask all these questions about me and never offer up anything about you in response."

Carlos quietly considered what I was saying, putting up a hand to shush me every time I tried to populate his silence with further prattling. At last he spoke.

"Well," he said matter-of-factly, "you never asked."

I scoffed with disbelief. Of course I had asked. Hadn't I? I shuffled through my memories of our interactions, searching for evidence of my reciprocal interest in Carlos's life.

"It's okay, Susan," Carlos said when I became flustered. "Most people like to talk about themselves. There are a lot more talkers than there are listeners. You're a talker, and I'm a listener."

I believed his words were meant to be reassuring, but I couldn't help but feel like a self-involved sack of shit. My default setting to fill the silence was always to yammer on about myself; it had never occurred to me to give him the same opportunity. My head was so far up my own ass, it was a miracle I ever saw daylight.

Sensing my growing self-loathing, Carlos gestured to the bag of M&M's poking out of my briefcase on the floor. "Hey, toss me one of those."

I complied, chucking the package across the office. In one fluid motion, Carlos caught the bag and returned it in my direction.

"No, open the bag and toss me one."

I looked at him, confused. "What, one piece?" He nodded. I opened the bag and shook out a single colored candy.

With an underhanded toss, I launched it into the air. Carlos wheeled his desk chair under the candy and caught it neatly in his mouth.

"There," he said, chewing with a satisfied smile. "Now you know my secret talent."

I chuckled, tossing him another candy. He leaned back in his chair and caught it. "What else do you want to know?"

I thought for a second. "What do you do for fun?"

"Nuh-uh!" Carlos admonished, pointing at the bag of M&M's. I dug another candy out of the bag and arced it across the office. He pushed off with his feet, wheeling his chair to arrive beneath the candy just in time.

"I swim with you," he answered as he bit down on the chocolate.

"Nice attempt at flattery, sir." I laughed. "What else do you do?" Another candy sailed through the air.

"I ride my bike. I run."

"Why?" More candy.

"I do Ironman."

"What's that?"

"It's a race."

"What kind of race?"

"A very long one."

Suddenly, I recalled him coming to work one Monday earlier that year, sunburned and limping. I hadn't asked him about it, but later that day, one of my colleagues had said he'd fainted in the faculty lounge. His wife, Diane, had been dispatched to drive him home. Was that because of Ironman? I asked. Carlos chuckled.

"Yeah. From now on, I'm skipping work the day after the race."

When I pressed for more information, Carlos turned his computer monitor in my direction and pulled up a website about the Ironman triathlon. I dropped the M&M's bag on the desk and leaned over to read the event description. My jaw dropped—a 2.4-mile swim, 112-mile bike ride, and 26.2-mile run, all in the same day? I had so many questions: Isn't that hard? ("Sometimes.") How long does it take you? ("On a good day, about 10 hours.") Are you fucking nuts? ("Depends on who you ask.")

"So wait." I paused, trying to make sense of what I was hearing. "You mean to tell me you suffer for 10 hours . . ."

"Yes."

". . . like, *major* suffering . . ."

"Uh-huh." Carlos nodded.

". . . and you do this voluntarily. For *fun*?"

"Yup."

"That doesn't sound like fun. That sounds like pain."

His eyes widened. "The pain is the best part! It lets you know you're alive!"

I scanned his face for any sign of sarcasm; there was none. This guy was actually serious. I could only shake my head and laugh.

"With all due respect, sir, I think you're crazy."

"I'm also hungry," he said, dangling the empty bag of M&M's, which he had finished while I was distracted by the Ironman website. "Let's order a pizza."

2 | WHEN THE SHIT HIT THE FAN

Shortly after our first anniversary, my husband asked for a divorce.

In hindsight, I should have seen it coming. For the last few months of our marriage, we were either arguing or avoiding each other altogether.

We got married because it was time. In our rural Wisconsin town, it was expected: love, marriage, babies, as soon as possible. Even for those who went off to college, it was generally expected that a mortarboard at graduation would quickly be exchanged for a bridal veil.

As a result, the decision to extend my education had not been made without criticism. "Don't you want to settle down?" my friends and family asked when I announced that I would attend graduate school immediately after finishing my undergrad coursework. "Have the wedding, buy a house, have a few rug rats running around? You can always go back to school when they're older."

I wanted to want those things. My friends were planning elaborate weddings and discussing family sizes, and I sometimes felt left out. My college boyfriend came from a large, tight-knit clan with traditional values, and I wanted so badly to belong. I wasn't particularly keen on the idea of babies, but everyone assured me that I would change my mind when I spawned a few of my own. So when my boyfriend asked me to marry him, I decided to get with the program. Two weeks after I finished graduate school, I donned the requisite bridal veil and said "I do" at the obligatory elaborate wedding. Love and marriage—check. It was time to settle down.

A month after our wedding, I accepted a position as a professor in Phoenix and moved across the country with my new husband. Our first night in our new house was also our first fight as a married couple. We fought every day for the next year.

Small-town Wisconsin was vastly different from big-city life in Arizona. I loved the bustle and unpredictability of Phoenix; my husband hated it. I loved my new job and the long hours of challenging work; my husband struggled to find a job he enjoyed. I felt like I finally fit in somewhere;

my husband stuck out like a sore thumb. He came to Arizona to settle down and start a family; I couldn't shake the feeling that I had just . . . settled.

I was convinced that something was wrong with me. If I just tried harder, I'd be happier. If I didn't work so much, he wouldn't be so unhappy. If I lost the extra weight I had gained after our wedding, he'd be nicer to me. Surely I was doing something wrong.

"I think I made a giant mistake," I blurted out one day while walking to the pool with Carlos. He looked at me with concern—the first time anyone had done that in months—and the levee of tears and anger and frustration broke. As tears began to stream down my face, Carlos took my arm and steered me back to my office.

"What's going on?" He closed the door behind him and pulled a handful of tissues from the box on my desk. I laid it all out—the fighting, the self-doubt, the unshakable feeling of failure. Even admitting feeling like a failure made me feel like a failure. Mostly, I cried. Carlos just sat there, listening and handing me tissues, until I ran out of things to say.

"So what do you want?" Carlos asked.

I didn't know. It was the first time anyone had asked me that question. I hesitated, then replied with what seemed like the appropriate answer: marriage, house, children. To even consider wanting anything other than that small-town bucket list of my youth felt blasphemous.

Carlos shook his head and inquired again: "No, not what everyone else wants. What do *you* want? You're allowed to decide, you know."

I didn't know. It would be a while before I really would.

My husband, convinced that a return to small-town Wisconsin would fix our big-city fights, persuaded me to move back to our home state for the sake of our marriage. We were happy in Wisconsin, he said, and we desperately wanted to be happy again. As the spring semester wrapped up on campus, I walked into my boss's office and handed him a letter. Carlos read my two weeks' notice and looked up with a disappointed stare.

After an awful silence, he said, "Is this what you want?"

"It is."

"Is it really?"

"Yes." This was not a lie. Well, not entirely. I wanted to want it.

"I don't believe you," he said frankly, "but I support you. If you change your mind, please know that you always have a job here."

"Thank you, sir." I walked hastily out of his office and made a beeline for my car, where I sobbed for an hour.

My husband got us to Wisconsin as quickly as possible, taking only what we could fit in our car. We abandoned any souvenir from our first year of marriage in Arizona.

As it turned out, we fought the first night in our new apartment in Wisconsin, too, and every night thereafter. The stress of the move only escalated our struggles, and a few weeks after our second cross-country move in the span of a year, my husband demanded a divorce.

I felt defective. Everyone around me had made love-marriage-babies seem so easy, and I had managed to screw it up in spectacular fashion.

But I also felt free. For some reason, "defective" didn't feel as terrible as I had thought it would, and certainly not as bad as I had been feeling up to now. If I finally accepted that I didn't fit the love-marriage-babies mold, maybe I could actually start creating a life that suited me. I was a rebel. A nonconformist. A devil-may-care *divorcée*, dammit. And even though I still wasn't sure what I wanted, I was going to allow myself to look for the answer.

The divorce papers were signed at 10 a.m. on a Thursday morning. I was on the front porch of my apartment by noon, drinking champagne straight from the bottle, when my laptop chimed with a new-message alert.

"Today is the beginning of great things for you," Carlos had written. "Go where you want and do what you want. Use this to get started with your new life." Attached to the e-mail was voucher information for the purchase of an airline ticket.

"I'm on my way," I typed in reply, smiling as I took another swig from my champagne bottle.

3 |

THE ANTI-DIET SUCCESS STORY

I only took up running because I wanted to shrink my fat ass.

There, I said it.

There's an unspoken agreement among runners that we're not supposed to talk about running as a tool for weight loss. We're supposed to "do it for the endorphins" or "fall in love with the journey" or other such motivational-poster crap, but honestly? A lot of runners started in the sport because they looked in the mirror and saw something jiggle.

I had a lot of jiggly parts.

After my divorce, I came down with a bad case of the Not-Enoughs. I had tried and failed at marriage. Despite my best efforts, I had hard evidence of my inadequacy as a wife, and I extrapolated that to all areas of my life: not pretty enough, intelligent enough, nice enough, industrious enough, funny enough, congenial enough.

To compensate for my shortfalls, I overcompensated. I returned to Arizona and threw myself into work, spending more hours on campus than ever before. I enrolled in a doctoral program, pulling frequent all-nighters to write the perfect papers and finish the perfect dissertation. I said yes to every work assignment and accepted every social invitation. Whether at a meeting or a party, I was always the first to arrive and the last to leave. In fear of letting down another person with my Not-Enoughs, I strove to be everything to everyone.

It was exhausting.

I tried and tried, yet I never felt satisfied. Every time I walked past a mirror, I'd groan and look away. I hated the way I looked, the way my belly mounded and my pants strained to contain my thighs. In addition to all my other shortcomings, I was not thin enough. I added that to my list of self-improvement projects for the future. Maybe I would start swimming with Carlos again. I hadn't been to the pool since returning to Arizona.

"What the fuck is this?" Carlos scoffed at lunch one day, taking from my hands the shaker bottle I was sipping, filled to the brim with neon-yellow fluid.

"Give that back," I exclaimed, scrambling to retrieve the single component of my lunch. "It's my weight-loss shake!"

His disdain for the weight-loss industry was no secret. "All you have to do," he'd say whenever I bemoaned my weight, "is stop putting crappy food in your face hole and do a little bit of fucking exercise. It's not that hard." I was quick to point out that he had never been overweight in his life. He had no idea just how hard it really was.

I knew. I had tried everything to lose weight: a week on a diet that consisted solely of diet soda and apples; a few miserable days on the Master Cleanse; an attempt at a cabbage-soup diet that ended with the first disgusting bite; diet pills and laxatives; restricting myself to 500 calories per day for a week, only to lose my resolve on Donut Friday in the office. I had taken every magic pill and read up on every secret diet, and yes, I could confirm that losing weight was hard. It was really, really hard.

"It's not," Carlos maintained. "You just need to find some physical activity that you enjoy doing every day. Weight loss is secondary. You really want to drink that crappy shake every day?"

(I did not want to drink that crappy shake every day.)

Carlos launched a campaign to get me to try running. Each day, he'd e-mail me another article aimed at beginner runners, and each day, I'd assert that I was not a runner.

I did not like running. Nor was I any good at running. Furthermore, I associated running with elementary school gym class, where we'd been forced to run the mile once a year while our gym teacher, Mrs. Morey, stood atop a hill with a megaphone and blared, *Yay, eagles! Boo, turkeys!* That experience had scarred this little turkey for life.

"Just try it," Carlos insisted. "I know you. You're going to be hooked."

"Running is *hard*," I whined.

"That's exactly why I think you'll like it. You need the challenge."

Grudgingly, and maybe just to prove him wrong, I decided to try things his way. At the gym one day, I hopped on the treadmill and turned the dial to a slow jog. In just a few minutes, I turned the dial back to a walk, red-faced and puffing.

Yep, it was confirmed: I did not like running. I was not good at running. It was hard, and I felt inadequate. Yet again. But like everything else in my life, the realization of this inadequacy led to overcompensation: I signed up for a 5K race. To prepare, I measured out a 3-mile route with my car and ran it every day, like a trained circus pony wearing a rut in the dirt. But quite unexpectedly, I found myself looking forward to this daily routine. The more I ran, the easier it got.

Perhaps running wasn't so bad after all.

When I crossed the finish line of that first 5K, I was bursting with pride. I couldn't wait to tell Carlos, who I knew would share in my celebration. Drunk with endorphins, I fired off a text with my finishing time and waited, giddily, for his response.

45 MINUTES FOR A 5K?!? My phone buzzed with his all-caps reply. WHAT DID YOU DO, SKIP?

Perhaps I had chosen the wrong person for a celebration. His callous reaction was crushing—I was not good enough. But I had to admit, it was provocative, too. I vowed to improve.

The goalposts moved with every race: training at a faster pace, then running a 5K under 30 minutes, then running 5-mile stretches in my workouts, then finishing a 10K race. Finish lines became starting points for new ambitions. I signed up for a half-marathon.

As each goal was accomplished, I slowly came to believe I was capable of accomplishing other, bigger goals. I felt a definitive—and unfamiliar —sense of empowerment growing with each mile run and each finish line crossed.

And just as Carlos had predicted in the face of my snide disbelief, along the way, I lost the weight and then some—almost 70 pounds in a span of four years. But I didn't stick with running for the weight loss. I did it for the endorphins, fell in love with the journey, and all that other inspirational crap runners talk about. As it turns out, those really are the best reasons to run.

There was no magic pill. There was no secret diet. There was just me and the work I was willing to do.

For once—finally—that was more than enough.

4 | ANYONE CAN DO AN IRONMAN?

Every now and then, my work would take me to cool places: presenting at a conference in New Orleans during Mardi Gras or consulting for a research project in Los Angeles. Other times, I'd travel to *really* exotic locales, like glamorous Coeur d'Alene, Idaho.

Technically, my meetings were taking place in Spokane, but a major basketball tournament had booked all the hotel rooms in town. My accommodations were 30 minutes away in a motel straddling an isolated stretch of the Washington-Idaho border. I was not thrilled.

"Wait a second," Carlos jumped in when I mentioned the upcoming trip. "When are you going?"

"Sometime in June, I think."

"Holy shit," Carlos said, laughing. "I'm going there in June, too!"

As it turned out, Carlos was racing his 10th Ironman in Coeur d'Alene the weekend after my work trip. Suddenly, Idaho didn't seem so bad. I decided to extend my trip to spend the weekend. I wanted to finally witness this Ironman spectacle Carlos had talked about for so long.

The morning of the race, I drove out to Lake Coeur d'Alene, where the swim would take place. I walked to the lakeshore, expecting to spot Carlos in the water. Instead, I was greeted by a mass of humanity in identical black wetsuits. I didn't know how many there were—more than a thousand, for sure. Possibly 2,000. I was floored. There were actually that many people insane enough to do this race? I had always thought Carlos was one of a handful of nutjobs.

The crowd buzzed with a quiet energy that grew as the sun emerged over the horizon. Something electric was definitely in the air. All around me, there were hugs and high fives and good-luck kisses before an announcer boomed through a microphone that the triathletes should take their marks: *Today, you are an Ironman!* Goose bumps prickled the skin on my arms.

The start cannon fired, and I watched the pack move into the water. I studied the expressions of the swimmers—determined, focused, even joyful. The spectators cheered wildly when they spotted friends and family members emerging from the water. I found myself cheering, too. I had no choice but to go along with it. I was overwhelmed. It was honestly so goddamned exciting.

I watched, riveted, for five more hours as the bikes looped through town. How could they stay upright for 112 miles? Carlos flew past me on his way to the transition area between the bike and run, flashing me a wave and an easy smile.

Then the rain came. As athletes made their way onto the run course for the 26.2-mile run, the sky opened up and drenched Coeur d'Alene with cold, heavy, unrelenting rain. I asked a spectator if they would cancel the race due to the storm. She looked at me oddly: "Why would they do that? This is Ironman."

It was confirmed: This sport made absolutely no sense. These athletes actually were insane. But I was impressed. I bought a poncho from a gas station and sat on the curb, awed, as I watched one athlete after the next run by.

"What are you doing out here?" Carlos yelled when he spotted me on the curb near the halfway point of his run. "Go inside!"

"No way!" I shouted back. I wanted to cheer until my voice was hoarse and clap until my hands hurt. It was a lot easier than what he was doing.

Runners came through the finish chute, wrapped in Mylar blankets to stave off the cold. Some fell to the ground, shivering and spent, after crossing the finish line. Some laughed, some cried, some just looked to the sky in amazement. I had never seen such pure displays of emotion.

And then there was Carlos, making his way through the downpour with a giant grin. Something about him was different. I couldn't place my finger on it, but I could tell those 10 hours had changed him. I was overwhelmed with respect and astonishment as he gave high fives to spectators on the sidelines and let out an energetic whoop of joy as he crossed the finish line. The race seemed to have given him an injection of vibrancy I had never seen before. But how? The race itself—140 miles in total—would beat most people down; the weather conditions certainly added to the suffering.

Then I recalled what Carlos had said the first time he'd told me about Ironman: *The pain is the best part. It's what lets you know you're alive.*

That was it: Carlos looked alive.

Later that night, he spoke animatedly of the day's events as he devoured post-race pizzas and downed a victory beer. Strangers, noticing the finisher medal dangling from his neck, stopped to congratulate him as they walked past our table. They were impressed. So was I.

"You're superhuman," I declared, shaking my head in disbelief.

Carlos laughed dismissively. "Anyone can do an Ironman, Susan. Anyone."

I turned those words over and over in my head later that night in my hotel room. As the events of the day replayed in my head, I thought about conversations I'd had with various participants throughout the day and realized the cast of characters really was diverse—they came in every shape, size, color, and age. There was a 70-year-old man doing his first Ironman. A young woman celebrating her 18th birthday by doing the race. A mother of seven. A man who had lost more than 100 pounds while training for the race.

Anyone can do an Ironman? *Anyone?* I opened my laptop and typed in a search query for Ironman races.

"Nah, this is insane," I said out loud to no one in my darkened room. I hadn't even run a half-marathon yet. I didn't know a damn thing about triathlon. What was I thinking, looking at Ironman races? I shut the laptop and tried to force myself to catch a few hours of sleep before my early-morning flight.

Anyone can do an Ironman. Anyone.

I sat up in bed and opened the laptop again. Turned out, there was a race in my home state of Wisconsin every September. I'd have just over a year to learn about triathlon.

Anyone can do an Ironman. Anyone.

I wasn't crazy enough to do this . . . right?

Anyone can do an Ironman. Anyone.

Count me in.

5 | SHIFTING

"You have got to be fucking kidding me."

Normally, Carlos took a day or two to reply to e-mails. Sometimes he didn't reply at all. Which is why, when I forwarded my Ironman Wisconsin confirmation e-mail to Carlos ("Congratulations! You just signed away a year of your life and all of your disposable income!"), I was surprised to see my phone light up with his text only moments after sending the e-mail. His skepticism took me aback.

No kidding. I'm in, I typed back.

Susan, this might be the dumbest thing you've ever done.

I slumped in my chair, puzzled. That was not the reaction I'd expected. Shouldn't he be excited for me? Proud, even? After all, he was the reason I even cared about this sport in the first place.

My phone buzzed again with a string of texts: Have you swum in a lake? Are you comfortable riding a bike for long periods of time? Do you even have a bike?

How dare he rain on my parade with logic? I'd signed up for an Ironman triathlon! Surely he could muster up some enthusiasm.

You're supposed to be excited, I texted back.

Jesus Christ, Lacke. You don't have a bike, do you?

I bit my lip and seethed. Sure, I do.

It wasn't a lie. I did have a bike. It was a mountain bike given to me by an ex-boyfriend for weekend trips to the bar. No longer would we need to designate a driver or call a cab for Sunday Fundays with friends, he'd said animatedly—we had wheels! Legal ones! Ones that would (mostly) stay upright after $5 buckets of beer!

So yes, I had a bike. Technically.

My phone buzzed once more: Well, then! Let's go for a ride next weekend.

Dammit. He'd called my bluff.

I didn't know much about triathlon, but I knew enough to know that my current good-time ride wouldn't work. I opened my laptop and began typing frenetically. My Google searches for the next 48 hours had a common theme:

> Can I ride a mountain bike in Ironman?
>
> What bike should I ride for Ironman?
>
> Triathlon bike

Cheap triathlon bike

Discount triathlon bike

Do I have to have a tri bike for Ironman?

Road bike for triathlon

Cheap road bike

Discount road bike

Why are bikes so expensive?

Oof. Bikes cost a lot of money. It was bad enough that I'd had to borrow funds from my mom for the Ironman registration fee. Now, it seemed I would have to drop significant dough on the gear, too. I had a serious case of sticker shock.

But it was Carlos's incredulity that rattled me to the core. How dare he call me out like that? He was supposed to be my friend, and friends support each other unconditionally. They don't laugh at big goals. Carlos was a jerk. I'd show him!

I muttered obscenities under my breath as I started a new Google search:

Credit card applications

Two weeks and several thousand dollars later, I drove to South Mountain, a nature preserve in Phoenix popular with cyclists, with a newly purchased bike in the trunk of my car. Carlos was waiting for me in the parking lot, leaning against his car with a smug smile.

"Well," he waved his hands with a flourish, "let's see the bike."

"Sure," I said, feigning confidence. I opened the trunk of my car and wrestled the heap of metal and rubber onto the sidewalk.

After hours of research online, I had decided my best bet for an affordable road bike was to purchase a used one. Following the measurements given on several cycling websites, I'd determined that my bike size was 54 centimeters. Only one had matched that size in a Craigslist search—a blue-and-white Specialized Tarmac road bike. The listing had a lot of information about components that made little sense to me but sounded impressive nonetheless. I'd driven across town one evening to meet the seller in the parking lot of a shuttered Walmart.

"That looks good," I said when he showed me the bike. "I'll take it!"

The seller's brow furrowed in confusion. "Okay, but . . . don't you want to ride it first?"

I took a few self-conscious laps around the empty parking lot with no idea what I should be looking for. The seller, sensing either naïveté or idiocy (or maybe both), gave me a business card for a local bike shop with some scribbles on the back: bike shoes, cleats, shorts, helmet, flat kit, pump.

"You'll need these," he said. "Go here, and tell them I sent you. They'll give you a discount." I gushed with gratitude, both for this stranger's kindness and for the new MasterCard in my purse. As it turned out, I needed both equally.

In the parking lot at South Mountain, Carlos gave my new bike a thorough inspection, crouching low to peer at the mechanical parts connected to the rear wheel. He looked up and gave a slight nod of approval. "Nice bike."

I puffed out my chest, relieved to have passed what I considered my first true test of Ironman training. I knew Carlos was a bike snob—he often bragged about his own ride, a fancy black steed designed specifically for speed and efficiency in triathlon. "Nice bike" was high praise. Carlos clipped together the chinstrap of his helmet and smiled.

"Shall we?"

We mounted our bikes and set off for a ride. I pedaled furiously, hoping I could keep my successful illusory streak going.

I followed Carlos to San Juan Road, an out-and-back stretch within the South Mountain preserve. I had run it several times before and knew the scenery well—7 miles of soft, gradual downhills into a valley, then a return trip to climb out. On the run, the uphill was a challenge, but I assumed it would be easier on a bike.

I assumed incorrectly. Pedaling downhill, my legs moved well, and I picked up considerable speed. After making the U-turn at the end of the road, however, it was quite the opposite. My pedals were suddenly lubricated with molasses, and my hamstrings were on fire as they tried to keep pace with Carlos, who was spinning effortlessly.

He looked at my slow-moving feet. "Why don't you shift down?"

My eyes widened. "No, I'm good, thanks."

"You don't look good. Shift down."

"Nah, I'm okay." The truth was, I didn't know how. I knew how to shift on my mountain bike, but it had numbered dials on the handlebars. This bike didn't have any dials. I wasn't sure what to do.

My legs continued to burn, and I moved at a snail's pace. Although I couldn't see him, I could feel Carlos trying hard not to smile. It was really pissing me off.

"You know what? Let's stop here for a second," he finally said.

We wove to the side of the road. My feet, shod in fancy new bike shoes that attached to the pedals, were stuck. At the start of the ride, the shoes had slid into the pedals with an effortless *click*, and I had assumed that unclipping would be the same motion, reversed.

Again, I assumed incorrectly. Still attached to my pedals, I fell over with a crash and a curse. Carlos doubled over with laughter, unable to catch his breath.

"Goddamn it, Lacke!" he said between loud chortles. "You really are an idiot."

My knee was skinned. The heel of my hand gushed blood. Hot tears stung my eyes. God, I hated bikes. I hated Ironman. I hated looking like an idiot. And I really hated Carlos Nunez.

"Really?" I huffed. "All you've done since I signed up for Ironman is make fun of me. You're supposed to be my friend. Why are you such a jerk?"

I squirmed my way out from under the bike and sat in the gravel on the side of the road, hugging my knees. Carlos sat down on the ground next to me, still chuckling.

"Why are you upset?"

"You called me an idiot."

Carlos, on the verge of laughter once more, took a moment to collect himself. "That's because you're acting like an idiot."

"Seriously?" I huffed. "You're still choosing to be an asshole?"

"Tell me the truth, Susan." He peered at me over the top of his sunglasses. "This is your first time riding this bike, isn't it?"

I hesitated, then nodded, trying not to cry. I couldn't keep up this charade any longer. As we sat in silence, I was certain Carlos was crafting new and creative insults to my intelligence. I was also certain I deserved every one of them. But, to my great surprise, Carlos wrapped his arm around me and let out a heavy sigh.

"You're really doing an Ironman, huh?"

I nodded again, the tears coming in full force. He was right: I was an idiot. Signing up for the race was the dumbest thing I had ever done.

"What am I going to do?" I wailed.

"Well," he sighed, "first lesson is figuring out how to ask for help. You'll need a lot of it if you're going to do an Ironman."

Carlos stood up, dusted the gravel off his shorts, and held out his hand to help me up.

"Second lesson: how to ride a bike."

6 |

IRONMAN IS HARD

In the year leading up to Ironman Wisconsin, I immersed myself in every opportunity I had to learn about riding a bike. And running. And swimming. And how to put it all together to make an Ironman. From my experience as a spectator at Coeur d'Alene, I had little to go on. Carlos chose to remind me of this often.

"You have no clue what you've gotten yourself into," he'd say. "Ironman is hard." For someone who derived such pleasure from this sport, he sure was full of doom and gloom. Instead of celebrating the things that were going right in my training, he'd pick apart my workouts and find something to improve. When things went wrong, he'd quiz me on what had happened, where things had gone south, what I should have done differently, and how I would keep it from happening again.

"Oh, come on," I protested one day, annoyed with the barrage of negativity. "Is it really necessary to look for the bad every time? I had a good bike ride today. Now, buy me a coffee and tell me I'm awesome."

"Buy your own coffee," Carlos snorted. "Your ride wasn't as good as you think."

Carlos never thought I was training hard enough; I thought he was a sadist. When high winds picked up in the desert, I'd rack my bike on an indoor trainer while he strapped on a helmet and headed outside. I thought covering 20 miles in a run was hard enough, but he insisted on plotting a course that crested every hill in Phoenix. He shoved his way into my lane of the pool during masters swim, deliberately jostling me with every stroke. Ironman training was a boot camp of exasperation, made more infuriating by his constant refrain of "You'll thank me for this later!"

Oh, I thanked him. Repeatedly, with my middle finger high in the air.

With six months to go before my first Ironman, Carlos headed to St. George, Utah, to race the Ironman distance for the 11th time. He insisted I come along. A group of our friends was racing, and he said I would take in a lot more from spectating this time around. I was now an Ironman-in-training, after all, not the casual observer I had been at Coeur d'Alene, and St. George presented an opportune chance to learn.

At dinner the night before the race, excitement and nerves were high. Eager to be the best cheerleader possible, I went around the table, asking friends for their estimated splits for the swim, bike, and run. Having that information would help me find them on the course to cheer them on. Appreciative of the fan club, they volunteered their best guesses. Carlos, however, refused to estimate his splits. He said it was an impossible task, since too many things could go wrong during an Ironman.

"Here we go again," I groaned. "Always the optimist."

All Ironmans are hard, but Ironman St. George had a reputation for being particularly brutal—a cold-water swim that could induce hypothermia, a bike ride with more than 14,000 feet of elevation gain, and a marathon with steep, unrelenting hills. To top it off, the weather forecast this year called for 100-degree temperatures and steady winds. It was a going to be a beast of a race.

So it wasn't surprising in the least when most of my friends came in well past their estimated times on the bike. The course and conditions were too hard to have a banner day. I was, however, surprised when Carlos still hadn't emerged, even after everyone else had come in. Of all our friends, Carlos was easily the strongest rider. He should have been first.

When he finally appeared in the transition area, he dismounted from his bike and limped to the changing tent. Confused and a little worried, I waited for him to reappear.

"It broke!" he yelled as he charged out of the tent and ran past me, still with a slight limp.

"What broke?" I hollered to his back. But it was too late. He was gone, running his way to the first of 26 mile markers on the course.

Soon, our friends began to cross the finish line one by one, exhausted but elated. "Where's Carlos?" they all asked, expecting that he would have finished far ahead of any of them. They were shocked to learn he was still on the course. Something was wrong—we just didn't know what.

Carlos eventually crossed the finish line, doling out high fives to spectators per usual. But instead of making a beeline for the throng of friends awaiting him, he collapsed in the arms of a volunteer. Within seconds, he was shuttled off to the medical tent. We rushed to the structure, looking for any glimpse of Carlos through the openings.

"I see him!" someone shouted excitedly, pointing to a cot in the back where Carlos was reclining. An IV was taped to one arm, pumping saline into his dehydrated body. The other arm was raised in the air in a thumbs-up gesture. A woozy grin was splashed across his face.

We got the full story when he was finally cleared to join us for a post-race dinner. Halfway through the ride, the derailleur on his bike broke, leaving Carlos stuck in his hardest gear. On the steepest climbs of the bike course, pedaling was all but impossible. His strategy was to ride up the hills as far as he could, then dismount and run alongside his bike as he pushed it the rest of the way to the crest. The effort of pushing his hardest gear, combined with mile-long uphill sprints while wearing bike cleats, wrecked his legs. During the entirety of the marathon, Carlos said he felt like he was dragging two concrete bricks.

Our group was aghast. "Why the hell would you do that?" we asked. Most people would have just quit when the bike broke. Although athletes are a stubborn bunch, clearly this level of obstinacy was new and unheard-of, even among my experienced triathlete friends.

But to Carlos, it was a ridiculous question. Why the hell *wouldn't* he do that? "I came here for a fucking challenge, and I got one," he asserted pragmatically between ravenous bites of pizza. Carlos tipped the neck of his beer bottle at his rapt audience: "This is what I trained for. Ironman is hard."

Suddenly, the Carlos Nunez sadistic approach to training made some sense. I was starting to discern that being a badass didn't mean performing well when conditions are just right. It was all about keeping your cool when everything goes wrong. And in Ironman—as in life—a lot of things can go wrong. You can complain and quit, or you can make forward progress. Carlos Nunez made forward progress, no matter the conditions, a daily habit. It was sadistic and smart all at once.

"Ironman is hard!" our crew exclaimed, raising drinks in the air for a toast. It was a story—and a lesson—we'd never forget.

7 |

VERY DUMB THINGS

It was one of those days.

Because I had forgotten to set my alarm the night before, I didn't wake up until almost 9:00 in the morning. Because I had gotten such a late start, I was riding my bike during the hottest part of a stifling summer day. Because I was riding my bike in the heat of the day, I was depleted. Because I was depleted, I was grumpy.

And because I was grumpy, I was *not in the mood to deal with Carlos's shit.*

And yet I had no choice. In my flustered rush to get out the door that morning, I had forgotten to grab spare tubes for my tires. I didn't realize my mistake until I was 40 miles out of town on a deserted road lined with puncturevine weeds. Their gnarly thorned seeds littered the road, creating a perilous obstacle course for my thin rubber tires. When I felt the telltale *thunk-thunk-thunk* of a flat, I plunged a hand into my jersey pocket and cursed as I realized my mistake.

I really didn't want to text Carlos for help. One of the first things he'd done after I bought my bike was teach me how to change a flat tire, stressing that I always needed to be prepared and self-reliant. "Nobody likes to rescue a dumbass," he'd repeat on a loop. "Never leave the house without water, food, or flat kit."

That day, I had only two of the three on my bike. I used my cell phone to text everyone I knew *except* Carlos, hoping someone would be willing to pick me up—but the replies ranged from Busy to No car to You rode your bike to where?

I considered my options: I could walk to the nearest gas station, more than 15 miles away, or I could wait for a car to appear on the desolate road, thumbing for a ride from a potential serial killer. Or I could text Carlos and admit that I had messed up. I looked up at the scorching sun and wondered if there was any benefit to befriending a serial killer.

An hour later, a black car appeared on the horizon, slowing to a halt upon seeing me on the side of the road. A tinted window rolled down, and the driver leaned across the passenger seat to take stock of the disabled bike and sunburned rider.

"For someone so smart, you really do a lot of very dumb things." Carlos sighed, unlocking the passenger door to let me in.

"I'm not in the mood, sir."

"What did I tell you? Never leave the house without—"

"*Not. In. The. Mood,*" I hissed. Carlos reached into the backseat and handed me an ice-cold bottle of water.

I never left the house without a flat kit again. But unfortunately, that wasn't the last time Carlos had to rescue me from very dumb things.

I was dumb tons of times, like when I read in a cycling magazine that losing weight would make me faster on the bike. I cut my diet down to a thousand calories per day, hoping a quick weight loss before that weekend's ride would make it easier to stay with the group without getting dropped. I lost five pounds before that Sunday and felt like I had won—I was smart. But when we started riding that morning, my legs suddenly felt and behaved as if they were made of concrete. Carlos pulled me from the ride, took me to Starbucks, and stuffed me full of whipped-cream mochas and maple-glazed scones until I felt like a human again. A very dumb human.

I was dumb when I declined Carlos's invitation to join a group of friends for a monthly practice swim in a local lake. "I prefer the pool," I said, and it was true. The pool was clean and the lanes well marked; I felt safe and capable there. It was the smart thing to do.

But the pool didn't fully prepare me for my first triathlon, a local sprint-distance race in which I entered the murky waters of the lake and proceeded to panic in spectacular fashion: *Why are these people so close to me? Where's the black stripe on the bottom? Why can't I see my hand in front of my face? What is that thing floating up from the bottom? That's a lake zombie. Oh, my gosh, that is a lake zombie!* I popped up in the water, frenetically doggy-paddling and gasping for air.

"Lake zombie!" I screamed. "Lake zombieeeeeeeeee!" Carlos, who was watching from the sidelines, doubled over with laughter.

I was dumb on my first century ride, during which Carlos yelled over his shoulder a reminder to eat and drink every 30 minutes. I rolled my eyes and retorted that I had things under control, *thankyouverymuch.* I didn't feel hungry, so I didn't eat, and—as I learned at mile 60—I didn't have things under control at all. Even then, I faked a smile and told him I was feeling fine despite the mental chatter blaring in my panicky, calorie-depleted brain: *This is it. This is how I'm going to die, in the middle of the desert wearing neon spandex.* Carlos, recognizing a bad bonk when he saw one, called for a break at the next gas station, where he silently handed me a cola and a bag of potato chips. It was unspoken yet clearly understood: I'd done a dumb thing.

I was very dumb two weeks before Ironman Wisconsin, when a nagging cold turned into a sore throat, which turned into an inability to swallow. I thought I was being smart by continuing to train, because I could sweat the illness out of my body through exercise.

One day after swim practice, Carlos suggested that we go out for frozen yogurt to soothe my inflamed throat. I jumped into his car with excitement, and he drove us a mile down the street and parked.

"This isn't the froyo shop," I stated, pointing at the brick building in front of us.

"Nope." Carlos got out of the car, opened my door, and gestured for me to follow him into the urgent care clinic. He did eventually take me for froyo—after the doctor diagnosed me with strep throat and wrote a prescription for antibiotics.

Even when he wasn't physically present, Carlos would still find a way to alert me when I was doing a dumb thing. When race day finally came around for Ironman Wisconsin, I did everything perfectly: I ate all the right things, did all the right warm-ups, and entered the water at exactly the right time. I paced myself well on the swim, fueled at the appropriate intervals on the bike, and started the run feeling strong and fast. I was dominating. I was smart!

In the early miles of the run leg, I saw my mom standing on the sidelines. With a concerned look, she waved me over to the curb and broke into a jog alongside me.

"Carlos says you're going too fast right now!"

"What are you talking about?"

She waved her cell phone in the air. "I'm on the phone with him right now. Carlos is tracking you online. He says you're going out too fast and that you'll pay for it later. Slow down!"

My jaw dropped in shock. *How had he gotten my mother's phone number?* "Tell him I've got this under control."

"He said you'd say that," she shouted as I pulled away to rejoin the main pack. "Don't be a dumbass!"

As I ran off in pursuit of the finish line—this time at a slower pace—I couldn't help but laugh.

8 |

ANYONE *CAN* DO AN IRONMAN (NO, REALLY: *ANYONE*)

Fourteen hours, 23 minutes, 42 seconds. On paper, it seems like such a long time, doesn't it?

In reality, those 14 hours, 23 minutes, 42 seconds of Ironman Wisconsin went by way too fast. It was—dare I say?—*fun*.

It didn't start out that way. The days leading up to my first Ironman were fraught with second-guessing. That anxiety turned into full-blown panic by the time I picked up my race materials the day before Ironman Wisconsin. Carlos had said that anyone can do an Ironman—hell, I had witnessed plenty of "anyones" at other Ironman races. But as I looked around at packet pickup, all I saw were people who looked a lot like Carlos—incredibly fit, incredibly confident, and with impeccable bodies. They rode expensive bicycles and ran in top-of-the-line shoes. They walked and talked like they knew what they were doing. They likely had never encountered a major health issue in their lifetime. The worst vice in their past was probably the occasional candy bar.

And then there was me.

I don't belong here, I texted Carlos in a panic.

Fake it 'til you make it, Lacke, he replied.

I certainly felt like a fake. When I set up the day before the race, more than one person commented on my unorthodox road bike, which stood out like a sore thumb in a sea of triathlon-specific rigs. I got a few incredulous looks when I said I'd only been doing triathlons for about a year. I was reluctant to mention much more about my life before triathlon for fear I'd get laughed out of the race. I felt extremely out of place, a 27-year-old former chubster in a sea of fit, middle-aged, overachieving men with rock-hard bodies.

Anyone can do an Ironman? *Anyone?* Heh. That statement was about to be tested.

I recalled Carlos's words yet again as I floated in the water before the start of the race. The sun was rising over the lake, and the scene was remarkably calm. As I looked around me, I remembered something from watching Ironman from the sidelines: Everyone in the water looked exactly the same.

In our black wetsuits, goggles, and swim caps, we were identical. Which meant that the thousands of spectators lining the shore would be completely and totally unable to pick me out of the crowd of 2,556 athletes in the water. I found this anonymity strangely comforting. At packet pickup, I was clearly different—I didn't belong there. On race morning, with only my head showing as I bobbed up and down in the water, I at least *looked* like a legitimate Ironman hopeful.

For a moment, I was calm. For the first time since arriving at the race, I didn't feel like a fraud. I think I even mustered a smile. And then the starting gun went off, and I was thrown into the thrashing mass, where the only thought in my head was a cacophonous loop of *oh shit oh shit oh shit oh shit oh shit.*

But eventually, the waves calmed, the bodies stopped bumping, and my arms and legs fell into a steady rhythm in the water: *Hey, wait. This isn't so bad.*

Don't get me wrong: It was challenging. Parts of that race sorely tested my abilities, and I used muscles I didn't even know I had. But considering that Ironman was supposed to be a sufferfest, I never really suffered.

Maybe it was because Carlos had trained me well in those months, weeks, and days leading up to race day. Maybe it was because I raced conservatively. Maybe it was because I had the support and love of my incredible friends and amazing family members on the course that day.

Or maybe it was because it's really hard to suffer too much when you run out of the swim and everyone moos at you (a tradition of the Dairy State's Ironman), or you have a crazy spectator in a pink Speedo or an Indian headdress running beside you up the hardest climbs of the bike course, screaming, "SUCK IT UP! DO YOU WANNA BE AN IRONMAN OR NOT?"

To my great surprise, I smiled and laughed as much as I grimaced over the course of those 14-plus hours.

At about mile 15 on the run, I saw a lot of people begin to hit the proverbial "wall." They were slowing down, rubbing their calves, walking, and sitting down at the aid stations. I braced myself for the same thing to happen to me. At about mile 20, I ran up beside an athlete who glanced over at me and muttered something I couldn't make out. I looked at him and asked him to repeat himself.

"This feels like death. God."

He dropped back and began walking while I kept going. As I looked at the trail ahead of me, I thought about what he'd said and took stock of how I was feeling. Death? Really?

I had never felt more alive. For years, I had woken up every day and used my muscles, bones, and skin without really thinking about it. I had never considered that the human body is capable of accomplishing amazing things. I had certainly never thought my own human body was capable of accomplishing amazing things. Yet here I was, checking off the miles under the power of my very own muscles, bones, and skin. It was an electric feeling.

As I turned the final corner toward the end, I encountered the bright lights of the finish chute. For 400 meters, there were hundreds of people, all cheering, yelling my name, and beckoning me to the finish line. Their roars reverberated through my bones. I let out a roar, too—it escaped my body with a tremendous joy I had never felt before.

I had started the race as an anonymous face among 2,556 Ironman hopefuls. When I crossed that finish line, I was an independent racer. I was someone who had achieved her goal.

I was an Ironman.

It no longer mattered that "anyone" could do it. All that mattered was that *I* could do it.

9 |

A TEST OF RELATIONSHIP FITNESS

When your best friend is of the opposite sex, dating can be complicated. When your best friend is someone like Carlos Nuncz, it's all but impossible.

"I'm going to set you up with a very nice boy," Carlos declared during a Sunday-morning ride.

I cast a skeptical look to my left, where he was riding. "He better not be a triathlete." I relished my new identity as an Ironman, entering more races and living a life in which I ate, slept, and breathed triathlon. But I would not date an Ironman. I had swum in that dating pool before, and it had ended badly. Many triathletes, I had discovered, were nice to look at but horrible for everything else. Arrogant and overly competitive, the men of triathlon were great training buddies and terrible life partners.

Carlos knew I felt this way, yet he often urged me to give it another try. Specifically, I needed to give it another try with the guys he wanted to set me up with: "very nice boys" from the local triathlon scene.

I ignored his attempts to play matchmaker, seeking romance elsewhere. I dated a forklift driver, a software engineer, a cop, a professor, a coach. Not one of them, blessedly, knew a thing about triathlon. But as much as I tried to keep triathlon and my dating life separate, the two would inevitably intersect. I'd cancel dates because I was too tired after a long run or eschew romantic weekend getaways in favor of 100-mile bike rides. If a guy managed to stick around through all that, he still had another hurdle to clear: meeting my friends, who were all triathletes.

"You look like you work out," Carlos said the first time he met the software engineer at a post-race brunch.

"Yeah, bro," he said. "I lift weights."

Carlos couldn't hide his amusement. "Oh, is that right, *bro?*" I kicked him under the table, but that only fueled his glee. Carlos peppered my date with questions about bench presses and clean-and-jerks, feigning interest before launching his first offense of the night: "I hear weight lifters have problems with small . . . well, you know." Carlos wiggled his pinkie finger in the air and nodded at my date's crotch.

The guy broke up with me that night.

Other times, Carlos lacked the patience to play the long game with my romantic interests. "You know what? I'm just going to say it," he sighed within five minutes of sitting down across the bar from my new love interest, a guy I'd met at a baseball game. "Susan, you can do better than this fuckwit."

Our crowd of friends fell silent. The guy glared at Carlos. I glared at Carlos. *Everyone* glared at Carlos. Yet he just shrugged, seemingly unfazed by the tension he had created.

The fuckwit's tires were squealing in the parking lot before our drinks even arrived. "Geez," Carlos quipped, leaning back in his chair, "so sensitive."

"Can you please try—just *try*—to be less of an asshole to the guys I like?" I said, seething.

"Sure, I can." Carlos raised his beer in a victory toast, gulping down his obvious self-satisfaction. "When you start dating guys who aren't losers. Have I told you about Brian from my triathlon team? He's a very nice boy. You'd like him." He took out his phone to text Brian with an invitation to join us at the bar.

"What part of *I don't want to date a triathlete* are you not understanding?" I stressed, smacking his phone to the ground.

But Carlos was undeterred. A triathlete companion would be competitive, yes, but I needed someone competitive to push me, he insisted, and maybe he was right. The guys I typically went for were clueless when it came to came to my lifestyle. A fellow triathlete would understand that I couldn't go out on Saturday night because I had to get up early for a ride Sunday morning (a recurring argument with several of the men I had dated previously); he wouldn't be offended that I needed to disappear for hours at a time to train; and most importantly, he wouldn't judge me for eating an entire pizza by myself after an 18-mile run.

"Also, he won't be fat," Carlos stated.

"I like big guys!" I protested. Carlos raised a skeptical eyebrow. I slugged him on the arm. "What? They're so huggable, like teddy bears!"

"A teddy bear who needs heart surgery in his 30s?" Carlos questioned, referring to the forklift driver. During our time together, he had required two stent placements in his coronary arteries—a direct result of years of cigarettes and a sedentary lifestyle—yet refused my offers to start exercising together or to help him quit smoking.

"He had his good traits, though."

"Susan, he was a loser," Carlos said. "Why can't you date a guy at your level? You always seem to find guys with nothing to offer. Now, a triathlete, on the other hand. . . ."

"Yeah, yeah," I said dismissively, motioning to the bartender for the check. I'd had enough of this conversation.

In my head, it was simple: Guys in triathlon (read: insanely hot) wouldn't like girls like me (read: clumsy and sometimes smelly). They were fit, driven, and healthy. Though I was participating in triathlon, I didn't consider myself a triathlete. The real women of triathlon were svelte, accomplished, and fast, and I wasn't any of those things. When I looked in the mirror, I didn't see someone who had lost 70 pounds or accomplished amazing feats of endurance; I saw the awkward, overweight chain-smoker I had been years before. I saw a loser. Turns out, the body can change its shape, but the mind is much less malleable.

Athletic guys had rejected me before I became a triathlete, and they would reject me now. Of this I was certain. Where Carlos saw a perfect match, I saw the potential for rejection: *You want me to be seen in public with her? Good one!* I imagined the guy sniggering before walking off with a slimmer, faster woman from my age group.

Then I met Neil.

The first time we saw each other, I was heading toward the finish line of an Olympic-distance triathlon while he was starting the run leg of a coinciding half-Ironman race. I had a flower from the roadside weeds tucked behind my ear; he was wearing his game face. I smiled and yelled, "Are we having fun yet?" He shot me a look that said, *Why the hell are you picking flowers at a race?*

But after the race, he approached me with a flirtatious smile, saying he wanted to know the name of the girl with the flower in her hair. I had a hard time believing he was actually talking to me, much less romantically interested. He was way out of my league—after all, he was a tall, chiseled, all-American type with a natural athletic ability that landed him on the podium at many of the races he entered. What I'm saying is that Neil was insanely hot, and I wanted very badly to touch his butt. Guys like him weren't supposed to like girls like me, but who was I to say anything about that? Blinded by butterflies and the possibility of kissing a good-looking boy, I accepted his invitation to meet for a cup of coffee later that week.

"No! No, no, no," Carlos said when I told him. "You can't date him!"

My face scrunched in confusion. "I thought you wanted me to date a triathlete!"

"I have some very nice boys to set you up with, yes," Carlos said. "He is not one of them."

"Is there something wrong with him?" I clutched my imaginary pearls, preparing to hear the news that he was a philanderer, an ax murderer, or worse—an Oakland Raiders fan.

Carlos pursed his lips in anger before leaning forward and hissing, "He's *faster* than me." It turned out that Neil had narrowly edged out Carlos in the finish chute at a race the year before. I tried—and failed—to contain the fit of giggles that bubbled up from my belly. It was all so ridiculous.

A few months after our first date, Neil and I were still going strong. One Saturday morning, I returned home from my long run to find Neil in my apartment. He was in the middle of a six-hour ride, and I'd told him he could use my sink to refill his water bottles.

"Hey, babe," he said as he leaned in for a quick kiss. "Good run?"

"Yeah," I said. "How's your ride going?"

"Pretty good," he said, turning on the faucet as I rummaged in the fridge for something to eat. "By the way, I saw your friend Carlos on the mountain this morning."

In shock, I bolted upright, hitting my head on the ceiling of the refrigerator. Until that point, I had avoided bringing the two of them together. Neil had no recollection of racing Carlos and therefore harbored no ill will; if anything, he found Carlos's contempt for him mildly amusing. The same couldn't be said for Carlos.

"Oh?" I chirped, trying to play it cool as I rubbed the burgeoning bump on my skull.

"Yeah, you were right about him," Neil chuckled. "He likes to throw his weight around. The guy tried to race me up the mountain."

This news did not shock me. "So who won?"

Neil looked at me with a confident smirk. "Come on. Of course I won."

It was typically triathlete—arrogant and overly competitive. It was also kind of hot.

After sending Neil off to finish the second half of his ride, I looked down at my phone. There was a notification from Carlos. I held my breath as I opened the text message:

Saw your boyfriend on the mountain this a.m.

Please tell me you were nice to him, I replied nervously.

Why would you say that? Carlos replied. I am always nice.

As I rolled my eyes at the absurdity of that statement, my phone buzzed again. He tried to race me, though.

Oh yeah? Who won?

Don't be ridiculous, Carlos replied. Of course I won.

A snort-laugh escaped as I typed my reply: Of course.

Neil was the first person to survive the Carlos Test of relationship fitness. And although Carlos could never quite forgive Neil for being just a little bit faster, he grudgingly grew to accept that maybe I had found a very nice boy after all.

10 | SQUEEZING THE LEMMON

The Santa Catalina Mountains rise majestically above southern Arizona, a stately crown atop the city of Tucson. The jewel is Mount Lemmon, a 9,000-foot peak that juts into the sky. Lemmon has legend status among cyclists for its 29 miles of unrelenting climbs lined with saguaro cacti and mesquite trees that give way to soaring aspens and ski resorts. At the top, a bakery in a cabin dispenses cookies and hot coffee to weary riders before they descend to the desert floor.

I had never fancied myself much of a climber. Despite a weekly excursion to ride South Mountain with Carlos, I never seemed to improve in my ability to ride inclines of any sort. Uphills were always a slog and a struggle. While friends seemed to get fitter and faster, dancing effortlessly on their pedals, I just barely got myself to the summit.

I was perfectly okay with this weakness in my cycling ability, however. Flat courses suited me just fine, and best of all, they didn't make me angry. I never once threatened to throw my bike into a ravine on a flat course.

Carlos disagreed. Naturally. And so it became his mission to find and unleash my inner mountain goat. He claimed that his intentions were to see me become a stronger cyclist, but I knew he just wanted another reason to ride Lemmon.

"It's time for you to earn your big-girl pants," he said one Sunday as we coasted down from the summit of South Mountain. "We're riding Lemmon next week."

"No, thanks," I said.

"It's a beautiful ride!" Carlos said, gesturing wildly as he talked about the stunning flora and fauna we'd see on our way to the summit.

"Not happening."

"It will make you stronger," Carlos argued. "Think of how much you'll grow from this experience!"

"Not interested."

"You'll get bragging rights," he said, puffing out his chest in a demonstration of swagger. "Climbing the legendary Mount Lemmon!"

"Nope."

"I'll buy you a cookie at the top. Two of 'em, if you want."

That got my attention. "Cookies?"

"Big ones." Carlos held up his hands in estimation of their size. "Bigger than your bike helmet."

I mean, I've done crazier things for a cookie. . . .

I capitulated. "Okay, fine. I'll do it."

As the week went on, I began to reconsider. The more I read about Mount Lemmon, the more I second-guessed myself. I had never even walked to the top of a real mountain before, much less ridden a bike up one. True, I had spent plenty of time climbing South Mountain on a bike, but compared to Lemmon, South Mountain's 6 miles and 2,000 feet seemed like an anthill—an anthill that took me a really, really long time to climb, by the way. I wasn't ready to tackle a challenge almost five times greater than that. Just the thought made me queasy with dread.

Can't make it tomorrow, I texted Carlos on Saturday night.

You're not getting out of this, he replied, unfazed.

To Carlos, a verbal agreement might as well have been a blood pact. He had zero tolerance for flakes—if you agreed to do something with him, you really had no choice but to follow through. Carlos didn't expect me to scamper up Mount Lemmon effortlessly, but he absolutely did expect me to show up.

Besides, he reassured me, Mount Lemmon really wasn't that difficult. I pointed out our greatly differing opinions on what constitutes "difficult."

Yes, but that's because you're a sissy, Carlos replied. I'll pick you up at 4 a.m. tomorrow, sissy.

The next morning, in a McDonald's parking lot nestled at the base of the mountain, Carlos polished his beloved bike while eating an Egg McMuffin and chugging a chocolate milk. I sat glumly on the curb, trying not to puke.

"Vomit if you want," Carlos said through a mouthful of breakfast. "You're still riding." He tossed a bag of hash browns into my lap and gestured at me to eat. I thought about what it would feel like to punch him.

The hash browns flip-turned in my stomach. Nerves amplified the effects of the caffeine in my coffee. Carlos whistled a lively tune as he unloaded our bikes from the trunk of his car. He was clearly excited to introduce me to Mount Lemmon. It was confirmed: I definitely wanted to punch him.

As we clipped in to our pedals and began the ride, my anxiety reached a fever pitch. A chilly gust flew down the mountain. My body was covered in goose bumps, partly from the wind, partly from fear. This definitely felt like a sign that I shouldn't do the ride.

"I can't do this," I said. "It's too hard."

"You're being a sissy." Carlos rolled his eyes. "Come on." He pulled slightly in front of me to diffuse the headwind.

The higher we climbed, the harder it got. Three miles in, the winds began to shift, coming at us from every direction.

At mile 5, I began to curse. We had been riding for well over an hour, yet it seemed we had barely made a dent in the mountain.

"Is it like this all the time?" I yelled over the howling wind.

Carlos looked over his shoulder and smiled reassuringly. "It's just a little breeze!"

A little breeze, my ass. That wind was cold and stinging. When big gusts came, I had trouble keeping my bike upright. I looked over the guardrail to my right and gasped—there was a steep, rocky dropoff to the base. People actually rode this mountain for enjoyment?

Those had better be some delicious cookies at the top, I thought.

About 7 miles in, we spotted a group of cyclists huddled in the corner of a lookout parking lot under a large tree. Carlos gestured to me to pull over.

"What's going on?" Carlos asked as he dismounted from his bike. The group looked at him with disbelief.

"You're kidding, right?" one said as he motioned wildly in the air. "The wind?"

A guffaw escaped from Carlos's mouth. "What, this?"

One of the cyclists pulled his cell phone from his jersey pocket and motioned for us to join their huddle. On the red screen blared an emergency alert:

> **WIND ADVISORY: MOUNT LEMMON**
> **STRONG WINDS ARE EXPECTED TO CONTINUE THROUGH THIS AFTERNOON INTO EARLY EVENING. SUSTAINED WINDS OVER 35 MPH ARE EXPECTED WITH GUSTS AS HIGH AS 55 TO 60 MPH.**

Feeling a not-small sense of satisfaction, I reached over and punched Carlos hard in the arm. *I knew this wasn't a little breeze!* He shook his head in astonishment. We really did speak two different languages.

Just then, a large truck pulled in to the parking lot. Leaning into the intense wind, a ranger from the Forest Service yelled at us to get into his car. We all threw our bikes into the back of the truck and wedged our bodies into the cab—a circus wagon full of helmeted clowns.

The ranger shook his head in dismay. "What were you guys doing out there, anyway? Who the hell rides their bikes in this weather?"

We all sat in silence, too shell-shocked from the ordeal to speak.

"Fucking spandex cowboys," the ranger muttered under his breath.

On the drive home to Phoenix, the silence continued. Carlos was shocked, I was angry, and we were both just plain exhausted. When he finally dropped me off at my house, he pulled out a small bag and handed it to me. Inside were several packages of cookies, surreptitiously procured from a gas station stop on the way home.

"Here," Carlos said. "These should hold you over until you actually get to the top."

It was the closest thing to an apology I had ever gotten from Carlos. I chuckled and gave him a hug.

When I got inside my house, I collapsed on my bed and took a three-hour nap. Upon waking, I opened my laptop and typed a Facebook status update on the day's events:

> Lemmon: The wind was below 40 degrees, above 50 mph, and I never, ever, ever want to ride my bike again. Ever.

I hit the "Post" button and scrolled through my news feed. As it turned out, Carlos had updated his Facebook status, too:

> Wonderful day at Mount Lemmon today. Sunny and warm at the bottom and a little chilly at the top, always with a constant gentle breeze.

Different languages, all right.

11 |

WELL, THAT'S ONE WAY TO WIN AN ARGUMENT

In 10 years of friendship, Carlos and I had only one real fight. We bickered (of course we did—he could be insensitive, and I was stubborn as hell), but we usually resolved our spats with a hard bike ride or track session interspersed with curse words.

I can't even remember the details of the fight. When we reflected on it later, I recalled a disagreement about a guy I was dating at the time, but Carlos was sure he'd said something about my bike to which I took great offense. Either way, the fact that we had such a serious disagreement is kind of embarrassing, especially since it led to us not talking for about a month.

As with the fight itself, the details of our communication hiatus are unclear—my version is that Carlos didn't return my text messages, while he insisted that I yelled something about putting him in "friend time-out" until further notice.

But as it turned out, the real reason we didn't talk for a month was because Carlos was in the hospital. Going about my business elsewhere, miffed and waging my battle of wills, I had no idea.

Then one day, my phone buzzed. `Need to talk ASAP`, Carlos texted, breaking a month's silence. `Meet for coffee?`

Not gonna lie—I puffed out my chest and chuckled arrogantly, proud to have held out long enough for him to crack. He was the one who'd given in. He was the one who'd reached out. He lost the fight; I won.

`Does this mean you're sorry?` I replied.

`Sure, whatever`, Carlos typed back. `Meet in 10, k?`

His brusque tone struck me. *He must really be having a hard time conceding defeat,* I thought. *I'll take it easy on him. Keep the gloating to a minimum.*

Carlos was already at the coffee shop when I arrived, tapping the table nervously. He looked tired and as if he had lost some weight. Nothing unusual; with an Ironman coming up in a few weeks, fatigue and pre-race weight loss were par for the course. I sat down at the table, folded my hands in front of me, and beamed graciously, prepared to receive his concession speech and get back to friendship as usual.

"I have cancer."

Those definitely weren't the words I was expecting to hear.

Looking down at a napkin he was fiddling with on the table, he began to explain. A few days after our fight, he had started experiencing stomach pains. He'd blamed it on gas from a new sports drink he was testing for his next Ironman. The following morning, he had been constipated. He'd blamed it on dehydration and upped his fluid intake during his 100-mile bike ride that day. The day after that, he'd become nauseated. He'd blamed it on a bug his kids must have brought home from school.

Nothing seemed to quell his nausea, though. He tried ginger ale and threw it up. He choked down Pepto-Bismol, and that came up, too. He couldn't keep anything down, not even water. Carlos went to the doctor, who sent him to urgent care, who sent him to the emergency room. There, they discovered a large tumor blocking his colon.

One day Carlos rode his bike 100 miles, and the next he had emergency surgery to save his life.

The tumor in his colon, about the size of an orange, was cancerous. The cancer had spread to his liver as well. He was classified as stage IV and given a prognosis of six months to live. He hadn't told anyone outside his family yet—he'd needed to wrap his head around it all before endeavoring to explain it to others. I was his first attempt.

With unsettling detachment and still looking down at the table, Carlos listed his treatment options and specialists. He explained his surgical scar with clinical restraint. He spoke unemotionally, as if he were a doctor describing some other patient in some other place. His composure was almost as disturbing as the news itself.

"So that's the story," he gruffly concluded.

I sat there, dumbfounded. This didn't make sense. He was sitting right across from me and looked fine. Shouldn't he look more sick? Wasn't he too young, too damn healthy, for colon cancer? How the hell had this happened? A million questions raged through my mind, yet I sat silent, too stunned to ask a single one. All I could do was stare at him, trying to comprehend what he had said. *You've got to be kidding me* was running through my brain like a news ticker.

Suddenly a lightbulb clicked on in my head. He *was* kidding me. This was some kind of sick joke. Of course! It all made sense! I began to laugh nervously. "You're messing with me, right?"

Carlos reached over the table and grabbed my hand, finally lifting his eyes to meet mine. During the entirety of our friendship, I had never, ever seen self-doubt there; I hadn't thought he was even capable of it. Carlos had always been so confident—cocky, even—but as he looked across the table at me, I saw something in his eyes I had never seen before.

"Holy shit," I whispered. "You're scared."

"Of course I'm fucking scared."

"I'm . . . sorry," I stammered, still unsure what to say. I averted my eyes and shifted uncomfortably in my seat.

"Hey," he said, squeezing my hand. "I'm going to fight this with everything I have."

When there's a 99 percent chance of failure, most people hope and pray to be in that 1 percent of success. Carlos said he planned to neither hope nor pray. Instead, he planned to *force* his way into that slim margin and own it, because that's what cocky people do. They suit up, even if it's a losing battle, even if they're afraid. And Carlos was afraid.

He was afraid that people would doubt his ability to survive. He was afraid he would pick the wrong doctor or select the wrong treatment option. He was afraid of leaving his wife to raise three children without a father. And, most of all, he was afraid of letting on that he was afraid.

He made the rounds—first with friends, then with colleagues. Each time he shared the news of his diagnosis, his rehearsed monologue became more convincing. After about a dozen repetitions of "I'm going to fight this with everything I have," it really looked like he meant it.

There were times when he showed cracks in his armor. At his first appointment with his oncologist, I saw his hands shaking so badly that he couldn't hold a pen to sign the required insurance forms. After a particularly intense round of chemotherapy, he could lose all conviction, weeping as he hunched over the toilet, vomiting.

In between rounds of chemo, Carlos and I traveled up to Flagstaff for a weekend of riding bikes. It was summer, and we wanted to escape the heat by venturing into the cool mountain air. Despite my efforts to start a conversation, he spent much of the three-hour drive fiddling nervously with the radio.

As soon as we arrived in Flagstaff, we changed into our gear and headed out for a long ride in the sunshine. Carlos was quiet on the ride, staring intently at the road ahead. I could tell he was tired—the recent surgery and chemotherapy treatments had taken their toll—yet he shook his head at every suggestion to take a break or ease up on the pace. That night at dinner, he sipped his beer silently and barely touched his food, looking ahead with the same intense stare.

"Well, good night," I said as we parted ways to our respective hotel rooms. "I'll see you in the morning." Carlos nodded tersely and turned on his heel.

Minutes later, there was a knock on my door. As soon as I turned the knob, Carlos pushed his way through and quickly walked into my room.

"I need to talk to you." His breathing sounded heavy and urgent. His eyes were wild.

"Seriously, man?" I threw my hands up in disbelief. "We just spent the whole day together, and you couldn't have—"

Carlos exploded, his voice almost a shout: "I want you to write a eulogy for my funeral."

"What?"

"When I die, write it. Say nice things about me. I want my kids to think I was a good person."

"Carlos, I—"

"Please." He sat on the side of the bed, looking at me with pleading eyes. I had never seen him so vulnerable. He had always been the levelheaded one in our friendship. Now, with the tables turned, I wasn't sure what to do. I took a deep breath and sat down next to him.

"You are a good person," I assured him. "The best. Your kids know it. I know it. Everyone knows it."

Unsatisfied with this answer, Carlos shook his head and glared at me. "Please," he said again.

I reached out and placed my hand on top of his. "You are not dying anytime soon, sir," I said with conviction. The doctor and his six-month prediction were wrong. They had to be. Three months after his diagnosis, Carlos was riding his bike for hours in the Flagstaff mountains. What dying man could do that? "We will worry about your funeral many, many years from now."

Suddenly, the worry lines on Carlos's face softened, giving way to an embarrassed smile. "You're right," he said. "I'm just tired. It's been a rough couple of weeks." Carlos gave me a hug, stood up, and declared that he was going back to his room to sleep.

He paused for a second before closing the door behind him. "Hey. Thanks."

"Anytime." I smiled. The door clicked shut just as my hands began to tremble.

If he could pretend to be brave, so could I.

12 |

MY MONEY'S ON THE UNDERDOG

The months following Carlos's diagnosis could only be described as a beatdown. A constant stream of surgeries and chemo kicked his ass. There were some good days, sure, but mostly there were bad days, really bad days, and occasionally *fuck-this-shit* days. But through the ups and downs, one thing remained constant: Carlos was a fighter.

Many fights aren't won in the first round. Sometimes there is round after round of fancy footwork and finesse, jabs and uppercuts. The fighters get tired and worn down as the roar of the crowd rises to dizzying volumes.

Then finally, in round 12, one fighter, wiping his bloody nose, sees a final opportunity and takes it.

A staggering, beautiful blow.

Sometimes the winner is the one everyone expected. The Alis, the Foremans, and the Mayweathers of the world are often a sure bet. But every now and then, it is the underdog who strikes that final blow, causing howls of shock in the crowd.

In the matchup of Cancer versus Carlos Nunez, I had my money on the underdog.

After Carlos's first surgery to remove the tumor from his colon, his doctor told him to use the morphine pump as needed and go for a light walk whenever he felt up to it. He'd be released in a week, the doctor estimated. Like a true triathlete, Carlos did what he called "track repeats" in the hospital hallways, pushing his IV pump all the way.

He was released from the hospital in just a few short days.

When a drug shortage caused his doctor to ration critical drugs and deny a lifesaving chemotherapy component to many patients, Carlos saw many cancer patients at his treatment center give up, believing there was nothing they could do.

Carlos refused. He wrote letters, made phone calls, and was a stubborn and tenacious presence in the treatment center until he was receiving his full chemo treatment every single time.

When the chemotherapy destroyed his white-blood-cell count, doctors told him he had to take a break from chemo treatments. Rest, they said, would be the only thing that would get his blood work back to normal.

Carlos did a sprint triathlon instead. It was one of his slowest races ever, yet he had a podium-topping smile the whole way. After crossing the finish line, he slept soundly for almost 24 hours. His counts were normal the following week.

Carlos's main objective was to live as normal a life as possible. Normalcy changed with every round of chemo, so he did what he could. When he was too tired to ride bikes, he'd be waiting at the coffee shop at the end of everyone else's ride for coffee and conversation. On days when he was too sick to leave the house for coffee, he'd e-mail to ask how a ride had gone. Even in absentia, Carlos was everyone's loudest cheerleader and toughest coach.

Cancer is a bully of a disease that aims to weaken and embitter. But for Carlos, it had the opposite effect.

"Have you eaten in the last 24 hours?" the nurse asked while preparing the latest infusion of chemotherapy drugs. Before every session, she ran down a checklist of the same questions, and it bored Carlos to no end. Why didn't anyone at the hospital want to talk about books or politics or what Jon Stewart had said on his show the previous night?

"Are you kidding me?" Carlos replied cheerfully. "I downed a couple donuts, a hoagie, and a few sticks of butter on the car ride over here! Chemo really works up an appetite!"

The nurse, unmoved by his attempt at humor, continued her stern-faced prep without even looking up. An IV needle punctured Carlos's skin. Dials were calibrated. "Uh-huh. Any health conditions we need to know about?"

"There's something you should probably know," Carlos stage-whispered. "I have a little bit of cancer."

Stern Nurse was not amused. "Noted," she said through pursed lips.

Tough crowd.

"Are you allergic to anything?"

Undeterred, Carlos leaned back in his recliner and grinned as the drugs began to flow into his system. "Sure," he said. "Kryptonite." From his recliner, Carlos struck a Superman pose, the wires and tubes of his chemo pump forming a de facto cape flapping in the wind.

For the first time in more than a dozen rounds of administering Carlos's chemotherapy, Stern Nurse cracked a smile.

It was the underdog's knockout blow.

13 |

WASTED

During the week, Carlos filled his days with hospital visits and pharmacy refills. But Sunday mornings were still ours. One Sunday, after the bikes had been put away and the coffee brewed, Carlos tilted his head to one side and looked at me with an astute smile.

"You know, you've really grown up since I first met you," he said, taking a sip of his mocha. "You're not such a fuck-up anymore."

"That's the nicest thing you've ever said to me," I said with a laugh, knowing how hard it must have been for him. The man could give an outstanding pep talk, but compliments were not his strong suit. I should have been flattered, yet inside I was cringing.

Because the truth was this: I was *still* a total fuck-up. I had just gotten better at hiding it.

I lied a lot. I lied when my boyfriend asked why I had been acting so strangely the night before; I lied when colleagues asked why I was late for work; I lied when friends asked, "We talked about this last night. Don't you remember?" And I lied when my doctor inquired about my drinking habits during my yearly checkup—*Oh, you know, just socially.*

I lied about my reasons for buying wine in a box, even though there is really no good reason why a single woman, living alone and drinking socially, should ever require a box-sized quantity of wine.

I lied about why there was an empty box of wine under my bed.

I lied when I was arrested for driving under the influence, blowing a blood alcohol level almost two times the legal limit.

And I lied a lot on Sunday mornings.

In my mind, dishonesty was a lesser crime than disappointment. I had successfully maintained the illusion that I could be all things to all people. In the course of a single day, I could be a stellar employee, doting girlfriend, loyal friend, and tenacious triathlete. I could have it all. Hell, I *did* have it all. My life was pretty great.

And I was absolutely convinced that this success was a cosmic mistake.

I feared the day when someone would realize my good fortune was a clerical error. It was coming, I was sure. I was not intelligent enough to be a college professor; I had only fooled enough people into thinking otherwise. I had a recurring dream of a representative from Ironman demanding that I return my finisher medals. When I went shopping for clothes, I grabbed items several sizes too large for my body. An e-mail from the editor of a running magazine, offering me a monthly column, was surely meant for someone else. Whenever Neil gazed lovingly in my direction, I wanted to grab him by the shoulders and shake him: *Wake up! Don't you know you can do better than me?*

This was not false modesty. This wasn't an *aw-shucks* when someone compliments your outfit or says you had a good race. This was a daily crippling fear that my life did not match the person living it. My case of the Not-Enoughs, which had crept in following my divorce, had advanced from a tiny whisper of self-doubt to a 24-hour klaxon alarm.

Wine helped. Plain and simple. That first delicious glass of red at the conclusion of every workday tamped down the volume. The second or third glass made me feel almost all right. Some nights, I was even able to achieve something that resembled relaxation. Then I woke up to empty bottles and dread.

Sometimes the mornings brought a headache or a bout of nausea that would go away after a run and a shower. Other mornings delivered intense panic. I'd scroll through my phone, cringing at embarrassing text messages or Facebook posts I didn't remember writing, or stumble down the hallway to discover Neil sleeping on the couch. I didn't recall him coming over to my place. I didn't know why he wasn't sleeping in the bed with me. I didn't know why he looked so apprehensive when he woke up.

The more I drank, the more I worried that someone would find out. The more I worried, the more I drank. I never intended to get drunk or drink myself into a blackout—I just wanted to feel all right. Sober Me resolved to have only one or two drinks; Drunk Me could never get enough. During my fugues, I'd polish off an entire bottle of wine and stumble down the street to procure another from the grocery store or gas station. As a precautionary measure, Sober Me started buying boxes of wine to keep Drunk Me safe at home. Drunk Me would polish those off, too. When it came to alcohol, my brain had no off switch.

My drinking was surprisingly easy to hide: If a college professor is tired, it's because she stayed up all night doing research or grading papers. If an athlete pukes during a workout, it's the result of giving it her all; no one suspects a hangover on a tough bike ride. I could still be all things to all people. If anything, I tried harder to be even more perfect in the daylight hours to offset my secret failures at night.

The problem with lying is that the truth comes out eventually. In my case, the truth came out one Sunday morning. The bright sun poured through a bedroom window I didn't remember opening. The room spun as I groggily cursed the daylight and tried to piece together the previous night: *Wine. I think I graded some student papers, too. Did I sign up for another race?* I signed up for a lot of races while drunk. I groped on the nightstand for my phone—it wasn't there, only a puddle of spilled wine. I rose and stumbled into the living room, where a figure was sitting on the couch. Had Neil come over last night?

"It's about time you woke up," the figure said, unmoving. I startled, sobering up immediately.

"Carlos?" I blinked with confusion. "What are you doing here?"

"It's Sunday morning," he said matter-of-factly. He was clothed in a cycling kit, his helmet on the cushion to his left. To his right was an empty box of wine. "I let myself in with the key you gave me."

"That was supposed to be for emergencies!" I grumbled. He had never just let himself in to my apartment before. I was angry that he had crossed a line in our friendship. Oversleeping for a bike ride didn't count as an emergency. How dare he?

Carlos handed me his phone and gestured for me to read. I had texted him at 11 p.m., claiming to be too ill to ride in the morning. I had texted him again at midnight, saying I had to go to the office to catch up on grading and wouldn't be able to make it to our ride. Between 1 and 3 a.m., I had sent a series of unintelligible letters. It wasn't the first time I had lied to get out of a Sunday morning ride, but it was the first time I had failed to successfully disguise the reason why.

Carlos, who had read all the messages upon waking, assumed I was seriously ill. He used his emergency key to let himself in to my apartment, where he discovered my body reverberating with snores on the bed. When he tried to shake me awake, I didn't stir. He was about to call an ambulance when he noticed an overturned glass on my nightstand and an empty box of wine next to the bed.

"What the hell is going on?" he demanded. I didn't have an answer. I knew there was no way I could come out of this looking good, but I certainly didn't need to look as bad as I actually was. The truth was too disappointing. I muttered something about having friends over the night before, even though I had actually spent the night alone. Carlos glared at me wearily. He knew I was lying. My secret was out: I was a fuck-up.

"Fine," he said, standing up from the couch. "Let's go."

"Go where?" I asked nervously.

"It's Sunday morning," Carlos sighed irritably. Wasn't it obvious? "Don't fucking think you're getting out of this ride."

That bike ride was the worst two hours of my life. My hangover symptoms were intense but paled in comparison to the pain I felt every time Carlos looked at me. I knew that he was finally seeing what I truly was: a drunk and a liar. The disappointment seared into my skin like a branding iron.

I never missed another Sunday-morning ride. I didn't want to disappoint anyone the way I had disappointed Carlos that day. I wish I could also say I never drank again after that, but in reality, the experience only made me a more careful liar. My drinking continued in secret for two more years, escalating until the day I woke up on the floor of my home covered in blood. At some point in the night, sometime after that second glass of wine, I had fallen and hit my head on a bookshelf. Terrified, I knew what I had to do.

"I need help." I shook with fear as I finally admitted the truth out loud for the first time. I divulged everything to Carlos: the drinking, the lies, the Not-Enoughs, the shame and guilt. He didn't say anything. He just wrapped his arms around me and held on tight as I fell apart.

I had feared telling the truth for so long. Yet in that moment, I felt relieved. My flaws were met with compassion, not rejection. With that admission, I felt like I could finally begin to create a life that matched the person living it. I didn't have to lie anymore.

The truth is this: I'm an alcoholic. And that truth fits me like a custom-made frock. It's not the garb I would have picked out for myself, but it's comfortable, and I can twirl about in it.

Sobriety hasn't been a magic cure-all. I'm still me, just without the box of wine. The insecurities are still there. Some days, the Not-Enoughs rattle around in my brain. It takes a lot of work and a lot of honesty, even when honesty makes me look bad. But I finally understand that my flaws don't make me a failure.

For the longest time, I thought Carlos had made me ride my bike that day as punishment for being such a fuck-up. But now I realize that wasn't the case at all. Just as Carlos had a backward way of paying someone a compliment, he also had a backward way of showing love. He was mad—the maddest I've ever seen him—yet he never gave up on me or on our friendship. The realization was profound: I can be a fuck-up and still be worthy of love.

When the Not-Enoughs creep in these days, I think of that moment of unconditional love from Carlos, and I don't feel so bad.

I actually feel all right.

14 |

LIFE AS I KNOW IT

Slowly but surely, I began to rebuild my life. I found that without drinking, I experienced a glut of both time and energy, which I used to throw myself full-bore into a burgeoning writing hobby. I had never considered myself a writer before, but a friend asked if he could post a race report I'd e-mailed him on his blog. That led to other blogs, which led to discovery by an editor at a national running magazine. He offered me my own column, to which I replied with a very professional question of "Are you high?" (He was not high. I still write the column.)

Triathlon was put on the back burner, my bike seeing action only on Sunday mornings when I rode with Carlos. For the remaining days of the week, I was committed to running, with a firm goal of qualifying for the Boston Marathon. I'd like to say this was part of a deeper plan for personal growth, and that is partly true. However, most of the impetus was purely financial. At an editorial meeting one day, my handlers knocked around an idea for their next bestseller: take an everyday schmo and create a Boston-qualifying specimen. Guess who was the biggest schmo on staff? It would be my big break as both a writer and an athlete.

Carlos was elated when I showed him my book deal. He said, chuckling to himself, "And to think, you didn't even want to run in the first place!"

He, too, was experiencing a rebirth of sorts: One year after being told he had six months to live, Carlos was still very much alive. He was tired, gaunt, and weakened, but joyfully alive. Better yet, he'd been informed that he was cancer-free. The doctors gave him the go-ahead to rebuild the body that had been ravaged by a yearlong onslaught of surgeries, chemotherapy, and radiation.

When we received the news that the cancer was in remission, there was much jubilation. There was gratitude. There were a few tears. Most importantly, there was normalcy. Carlos took to track workouts with gusto and convinced me to fold some swim workouts with him into my Boston training plan. Racing was on his radar, too: "If I'm still in remission at my next checkup, I'll register for a 5K."

With a mischievous grin, he leaned in and whispered, "And who knows? Maybe I'll do another Ironman someday."

I had my best friend and training partner back. Life as I knew it had returned.

The bliss was short-lived.

Four months after being declared cancer-free, Carlos texted me from his doctor's office: 2 tumors in liver. Surgery not an option.

It felt like someone had reached through my phone and punched me hard in the gut. Things had finally returned to normal, only to be upended all over again.

A few days later, over lunch, he described the size and location of the tumors and what it meant for the future: "It looks like my options are pretty limited, but we'll give them all a shot. Don't close the book on me just yet. I've got a feeling there's still a few more chapters left."

I smiled. "Yes, there are."

"I asked my doctor if he thought I could still do a triathlon. He said he didn't see why not."

"Of course," I said, mirroring his optimism and thinking of an upcoming local sprint that would be perfect to train for together. "Might as well!"

"So I'm going to sign up for Ironman Arizona."

I choked on the sip of water I had just taken. "What?" I sputtered.

Carlos flashed that grin I had come to associate with his mischief during the seven years of our friendship. "You in?"

The timing couldn't have been worse. I was knee-deep in training for a Boston qualifier, which was ridiculously far out of my comfort zone. I had already announced this goal to the readers of my column. The ink on my book contract was barely dry. I had deadlines to meet for the magazine each week. I was still teaching full-time. There was no way I could train for a long-distance triathlon—no way. An Ironman simply did not fit into my plans.

I looked at Carlos's eager expression. "Yeah," I said. "I'm in."

Boston could wait. I needed to train for Ironman Arizona first.

There was a lot I didn't know. I didn't know how Carlos would handle training for an Ironman on top of the rigors of cancer treatment. I didn't know how the doctors would treat Carlos this time around, or if it would even work. I didn't know how much time he, or I, or anyone else had left on this planet. But what I did know was that if some of his precious time was going to be spent training for an Ironman, there was no place I wanted to be more than on his back wheel every Sunday.

Life as I knew it had returned.

15 |

SUNDAY MORNINGS

With Ironman Arizona on thc horizon, our Sunday-morning bike rides became more important than ever. Though we agreed that the rides themselves were critical, Carlos and I would often bicker over the details. Every Saturday, we kicked off our weekly haggle over our Sunday-morning ride with a series of text messages:

Me: Riding 3 hrs tomorrow, S. Mountain. Leave at 9 a.m.

Him: Leave at 7 a.m.

Mc: It's cold at 7! 9.

Him: Not that cold. 7.

Me: Compromise, meet at 8?

Him: Quit whining, 7.

Me: You're an asshole.

Him: Love you, too, see you at 7.

On Sunday morning, I'd drag myself out of bed early and chug several cups of coffee before riding to meet Carlos in a parking lot midway between our houses.

"Can you take it easy on me today?" I would always ask.

"Of course," Carlos would always reply, smiling.

Let the record show that Carlos Nunez is a big, fat liar.

One would think multiple rounds of chemotherapy and several intensive surgeries would slow a man down. At least, that was my logic when I decided to train with him for this Ironman: *He's been through a lot, but hey! Silver lining! He's probably slow enough that I can finally keep up with him on the bike!* (Yes, these thoughts confirm that I am a terrible, horrible, no-good, very bad friend.)

As it turns out, not only was I awful but my logic was not sound.

Those Sunday rides were humbling. Sometimes so humbling that I would threaten to throw my bike off the side of the mountain.

"You're supposed to be sick, dude," I would wheeze while trying to keep up with him. "Act like it."

"And you're supposed to be in shape," he would retort. "Act like it."

After a particularly rough Sunday on the bike, I came home to several text messages from elated friends, all of whom had qualified for Boston at a local marathon that day. Though I felt bad for even thinking it, I resented giving up my own marathon training in order to struggle behind Carlos every Sunday. I couldn't help but wonder if I had made the right decision by signing up to do another Ironman triathlon. Though I was ashamed of my selfishness, that night, I surreptitiously browsed marathon websites, the way a husband looks at pornography websites after his wife goes to bed.

The following weekend brought yet another round of text messages between Carlos and me and another early-morning Sunday meet-up in the cold. We rode our familiar route in our familiar way, with me huffing and puffing as he pulled farther away from me on the mountain. As always, the ride became a game of hide-and-go-seek: I'd turn a corner, and there he'd be, dancing on the pedals, seemingly without effort, a few hundred yards in front of me.

When I finally reached the top, Carlos was waiting for me. He pointed at his watch and shrugged quizzically, as if to say, *What took you so long?* I pointed, too, with my middle finger. He laughed as he rolled out toward the descent.

If you've never ridden your bike down a mountain, you're missing out. The contrast of the pain going up and the effortless speed going down creates pure, childlike joy. You can't help but have a big, stupid grin on your face. There is no better feeling in the world than flying down a mountain on a bike.

That is, until you get to the bottom and see an identical grin on your best friend's face—a grin you'd once feared you'd never see again.

Suddenly, I remembered exactly why I was training for this Ironman. This decision had nothing to do with the actual race. It had nothing to do with bikes, nothing to do with humility, and nothing to do with Boston.

It had everything to do with Sunday mornings and big, stupid grins.

As we headed toward home, the sun warmed our wind-burned cheeks and numb fingers. I looked to my left, where Carlos was riding, still grinning.

"Hey, sir?"

"Yeah?"

"I'm glad we're doing this."

"Me, too."

"Next week?"

"Yes. Seven a.m."

"Nine a.m."

"Seven."

"You're such an asshole."

"I love you, too."

16 |

DAVID & GOLIATH

As dear a friend as he was, and despite everything he had done for me, I couldn't repay Carlos with the one favor he requested.

"Come on," Carlos whined. "You owe me."

"That is true," I nodded in agreement, "but I can't do this."

Carlos pushed the laptop across the table and positioned its keys under my fingers. "This should be the easiest thing ever. You're a writer. It's what you do. Now, write for me."

At the one-year mark of Carlos's diagnosis, his college had decided to honor him with a lifetime achievement award. Carlos balked at the attention, believing his life was hardly remarkable.

"They want me to give a speech!" he said, laughing. "They said I'm inspiring! Me! Ha!" He gestured at the computer again. "Go ahead, make something up. I have nothing interesting to say."

"You're the most interesting person I know," I asserted, pushing the computer back to his side of the table.

"I'm a shitty writer," Carlos moaned.

"Just write something. Anything," I coaxed. "Give me a draft, and I'll help you clean it up. Sound good?"

I didn't hear much from him for the next two weeks, aside from the occasional frustrated text message (Writing is stupid. I sound like an idiot. I'll pay you to write this for me.) The day before the awards ceremony, Carlos requested an emergency coffee date.

"It's as good as it's going to get," he sighed, opening the computer. As I quietly read the speech, he winced in anticipation of my editorial critique.

The screen began to blur as tears formed in my eyes.

"It's perfect," I whispered.

And it was.

I am not here for pleasant conversation.

I am here to tell you about things that happen to people—bad people and good people. Things that make some cry and question life's fairness and God's existence. But it's okay, because I know I am in good company. Many of you have likely gone through hell and back. I know, like you, how it feels being in pain, scared, hopeless, helpless, defeated, cheated, and alone.

But I also know we are made of some tough stuff. Every one of us is equipped to climb over obstacles. We are all made to fight and never give up.

A year ago, I was what people call "super-fit." My sport makes regular people cry in pain just watching it on TV! Ironman consists of swimming 2.4 miles, biking 112 miles, and then running 26.2 miles, a full marathon, in less than 16 hours. I have done this 13 times in races across the United States and Europe.

I was in the midst of training for yet another Ironman last April when I suddenly got sick. It wasn't a gradual, progressive illness. One day I rode my bike for 6 hours, and the next I had emergency surgery. In an instant, everything changed.

One year ago, I was told that I had stage IV colon cancer, the most advanced stage of cancer.

The tumors in my colon had metastasized to the lymph nodes and to the liver. With luck and chemotherapy, every oncologist said I could live another year, but the odds of survival beyond that were slim. Liver surgery is an option for some with my cancer, but I was not a candidate for it, as I had too many tumors.

The doctors didn't say it outright, but I could tell what they were thinking: Start writing your will.

I was in denial. I sought a second and a third and a fourth opinion. This type of thing shouldn't happen to me. This is a disease that affects old people, the overweight, the sedentary, the smokers. There is no cancer in my family history. I am 20 years younger than the average colon cancer patient.

After being diagnosed with cancer, my main concern was how to break the news to my 10-year-old son. The prospect was daunting: How do I tell my son that his father is going to die soon? I took him for a walk but it was difficult to even touch the subject.

"Dad, are you going to die?" he asked.

I tried to be philosophical: "We are all going to die, son."

He replied, "Yeah, but you know what I mean."

I couldn't lie anymore. "I have a very, very serious, dangerous, mean disease that kills many people."

Without flinching, he looked at me. "Yeah, but you will fight it, right? You will beat it, I know you will."

It broke my heart. "I promise you, I will fight this harder than anybody in the world has fought it, I will always fight, I will never give up, and I will never be afraid of it."

"You promise?"

"I promise."

"Dad, I think you are going to be the first person to beat cancer and finish an Ironman!"

And that was it. If he could believe and hope for the best, so could I. I decided then that I was going to fight cancer with everything I had.

I asked my oncologist for the most toxic chemotherapy poison he had, and to double the dose. He smiled at me and said, "Look, I'm an aggressive oncologist, but we want to kill the cancer, not you."

We made an agreement: As a symbolic gesture to this fight I was going to start, he was going to change the goals of chemotherapy in the medical record. My file originally said, "Goal: Palliative care, to extend life."

He scratched that out and made a new entry: "Goal: To cure."

Chemotherapy was a bitch. Sorry, but that's the only one word I can use to describe it. During those 6 months, I didn't feel like I was getting better; I felt I was just dying faster. Fatigue, pain, nausea, insomnia, constipation, loss of motor function, permanent numbness of hands and feet, rashes; you name it, I had it.

A blood test in month four of chemotherapy revealed the worst: Chemotherapy was not working. I was going to die.

I drove to Mexico that night to say goodbye to my parents and my brothers and sisters . . . but halfway there, I turned around. I was ashamed of myself. This was not fighting; this was giving up. And I made a promise to my son that I wouldn't do that.

That night at home, I wrote in my journal and to my friends on Facebook:

> The other day, I read an article picking apart the credibility of the David and Goliath biblical story. Could a teenage boy with a sling and stones really have killed a well-armored, trained-to-kill warrior?
>
> It was a funny question, I thought. Davids have been slaying Goliaths for centuries! Every day all over the world, people like us, little Davids, get up in the morning and beat giants against all odds.
>
> Tonight I have decided that I am David, and cancer is my Goliath.

It's a huge opponent, an experienced, mutant killer. This fight is being held in a coliseum, and I don't want to be here.

But Goliath is not well liked, you know? He doesn't have a fan base. All the spectators in this coliseum have taken my side, and that makes a difference. They seem to think I am special, stronger, tougher than I actually am. It gives me pride, and for them, I can't quit. I am not fighting alone.

In spite of the bad news that the chemotherapy wasn't working, I continued anyway, never missing a session even when I felt like I couldn't take it anymore.

Five months into chemo, a new CT scan showed some tumors shrinking. By the end of my six-month chemo treatments, I had learned many tumors had shrunk in size, and many more were dormant.

Because I had fought, because I had stuck with it, the liver surgery that was impossible six months before was now possible. I had the first surgery on December 29th, the second on January 5th.

Then, on February 7th, after a seven-and-a-half-hour surgery, I was cancer-free.

It's not over completely. I still have three months of chemotherapy left, beginning Thursday. I have to tell you, I cannot wait to start. I am going to own these four rounds of chemo. I did over six months before, and three months pales in comparison. This is going to be cake!

There is a chance that cancer will come back: a 60 percent chance that it will come back in one year and a 75 percent chance that it will come back in five years. If it happens, I guarantee you I will fight it again.

Cancer may destroy my body slowly, entirely, and definitely. But through it all, cancer will not touch who I am.

Cancer can take away my ability to run really hard in the mornings. But it cannot take away my ability to enjoy the last few stars before sunrise while I slow-jog and walk. It may one day take away my weekend bike rides with my friends up my favorite mountain and the breakfast after. But it cannot take away the camaraderie and love we feel for each other. Cancer has already taken away my ability to swim in the evenings, but the love of the sport doesn't go away. I still dream of swimming, and in my head I am Michael Phelps. Cancer has taken away, more than once, my enjoyment of a restaurant dinner with my family when I had to run to the bathroom to puke . . . but it cannot take away my love for them or their love for me.

Cancer can destroy my colon, take away my liver, clog my kidneys, and choke my lungs, but through it all, I refuse to let it grab hold of my heart or destroy my mind. Cancer won't make me a bitter person before it kills me. Cancer can destroy me, but it will not defeat me.

I may not be strong enough to put my son on my shoulders anymore, but cancer won't ever take away the walks we already had together, when he held my hand and in his mind there was no one stronger than I, when he thought I was untouchable, indestructible.

Cancer cannot win. It will not win.

Whatever your fight is, when you are thrown into the coliseum to fight, you become a gladiator, too. Half naked, with nothing but stones and a borrowed sword.

If cancer comes back, it will be more aggressive, meaner, mutated. Honestly, I am not worried anymore.

I am little David, and cancer is my Goliath.

And we all know how the story ends.

17 |

LIFE'S TOO SHORT TO GO SO FUCKING SLOW

"You can drop me, you know." I let out a loud breath as I shifted gears on my bike.

"Don't be ridiculous, Susan," Carlos replied with a smile. "I'm not dropping you."

"I'm serious. Go ahead, I'll meet you at the top of the mountain."

But Carlos stayed by my side, relaxed and taking in the scenery around him. This was his new *thing*, he said: riding for fun, not for a PR at Ironman Arizona. Cancer, he said, had given him a new perspective on what was important in life.

Part of me believed him. But another part of me knew—and was trying hard to ignore—the reality. Every week, it was becoming easier to keep up with Carlos. Some days, he'd even gesture for me to ride in front of him.

"You're fit enough to take a pull now and then," he'd say gallantly.

I was not fit enough. I was never fit enough. Still, I'd hop to the front and let him sit in my draft.

Ten months before Ironman Arizona, the scar tissue from four liver and lung surgeries made it too uncomfortable for him to ride his tri bike, which demanded that he bend at the torso where his surgical incisions were still healing. This was upsetting for him; he adored that bike. But never one to accept defeat, he bought a road bike, which allowed him to ride in a more comfortable upright position. I started to take more pulls, enough to warrant the purchase of a rearview mirror to keep an eye on him.

With eight months to go before our Ironman, the frequency of our rides together declined as his chemotherapy increased. When we did ride, he was tired, gaunt, and pale. I spent most of those rides checking on him in my rearview mirror and making sure I was giving him enough of a draft. This change in pecking order was difficult for both of us—Carlos had always been such a robust rider, yet now he struggled to maintain even the slowest pace. In our new style of riding, I never knew which was more important to protect—his body or his pride.

But glimpses of strength would sometimes appear, usually in the form of his middle finger in my rearview mirror. I loved seeing that. That gesture of defiance made me feel like everything was still normal, that within that worn-down physical body was a brain that was still capable of telling me to stop being a dumbass.

Seven months before Ironman, the doctors pumped the brakes on treatment. The chemotherapy was incredibly effective at killing the cancer, but it was even more effective at killing the healthy cells in his body. The treatments had created a shell of a man—he wasn't eating, he could barely sleep through the pain, and his hands and feet had become numb with neuropathy. His white-blood-cell count was almost nonexistent, and opportunistic infections kept landing him in the hospital.

"All this work trying to beat cancer," he'd joke under his breathing mask, "and I'm getting taken out by the common cold."

Then something amazing happened—with the cessation of the chemotherapy treatments, the old Carlos returned in full force. Food was appealing again, he clocked a solid eight hours of sleep per night, and the color came back to his face.

Riding tomorrow, Carlos texted me one Saturday night. It had been almost a month since he had ridden. I felt joy swell up in my chest and went immediately to the garage to reinstall the mirror on my bike.

He showed up in the parking lot between our houses the next morning, ready to ride. And boy, was he *ready*: I had barely rolled in on my bike when he gestured to South Mountain and led the way out at breakneck pace.

Carlos was so happy, so fully *alive*, that he barely noticed or cared that I was struggling to keep up. For the first time in months, he was the one decelerating to keep the slower rider on his wheel. The order of things felt right again.

Struggling to stay close, I wheezed, "Go ahead! Don't let me hold you back."

"Nah, this is a nice, relaxing pace." (Did I detect a hint of smugness?) "I'm riding for fun, anyway." (Pretty sure that was smugness.) I put my head down and tried to stay on his wheel, refusing to sandbag this torrent of energy. Carlos started whistling a jaunty tune. (Definitely smugness.)

As we climbed farther up the mountain, both my speed and his patience waned.

"Oh, for fuck's sake, Lacke," sighed Carlos as he stood up out of his saddle and pedaled away from me, "life's too short to go so fucking slow."

I rolled up to the top of the mountain 20 minutes later. Carlos was straddling his bike frame, leaning on the handlebars as he scrolled through the Facebook feed on his phone—he had been at the summit long enough to get bored. As soon as our eyes met, we exploded with hilarity. I don't think either of us had laughed that hard in a long time.

Over post-ride coffees, Carlos talked animatedly about resuming his training for Ironman Arizona. If he could feel this good for the next six months, he'd have more than enough in the tank to complete the race.

The old Carlos had bounced back. It was thrilling. Yet amid the laughter, the planning, and the big talk, we both suspected it might be fleeting. Eventually, even the highest bounces must return to Earth.

And this one did.

Although we didn't know it at the time, that morning was the last time we'd ever ride together. We had plotted a return to regular Sunday rides, but his body made other plans. In rapid succession, there were surgeries—on his heart, to remove blockages caused by the chemo port that had fed the medications into his bloodstream; ablations followed, to remove the tumors that returned to his body like invasive weeds during the absence of chemotherapy drugs. A tumor-filled wedge of his liver was removed. More than 20 rounds of chemotherapy followed.

Our rides together were off, but Sunday mornings were still very much on as I continued my Ironman Arizona training alone. Each week, I'd finish my ride and head to Starbucks, where Carlos would be waiting to swap battle stories. I'd tell him about bonking 60 miles into my ride, and he'd scold me for making stupid mistakes in my eating schedule. He'd tell me he'd walked around for four hours after invasive surgery, and I'd yell at him for being a show-off for the nurses when he should have been resting.

He said he missed our Sunday-morning rides. I missed them, too.

In his absence, I tried riding with other friends, but it wasn't the same. Even in a peloton, I felt alone. The plan was for Carlos and me to train for Ironman Arizona together, and I felt sad and even guilty about riding without him. So instead, I'd ride my bike to the parking lot midway between our houses and wait for a minute before rolling out—just in case.

***

One hundred days before Ironman Arizona, I broke my bike. It was a stupid, random occurrence but a debilitating one. A crack in the frame rendered it unsafe to ride, and I scrambled to find an affordable replacement.

That Sunday over coffee, I was lamenting my lack of options to Carlos. A new bike was too expensive. A used bike was also too expensive. I wondered aloud if putting Super Glue on my fractured bike frame would really be all that dangerous.

"You fit on a 54-centimeter bike, right?" Carlos interjected.

"Yes," I replied. "Why?"

"Take my tri bike."

The offer gave me pause. That tri bike was his most prized possession. Carlos loved it so much that whenever anyone got near it, he'd wedge his body defensively in front of the frame. No one touched his bike—ever.

"Take my tri bike," he repeated. "Swap out the pedals, get a fit at the shop, and make any adjustments you need to make."

I knew I had to ask the question we had avoided for so long. "But what about Ironman?"

"The doctor wants me to do more chemo. I can't do the race."

We sat in silence, uncomfortable with the reality we had tried so hard to avoid.

"Take my bike. Do our Ironman. You'd better go fast, though. . . ."

I smiled knowingly as I finished his sentence in my head: *Life's too short to go so fucking slow.*

That day, I finally accepted that I wouldn't be spending my training days chasing Carlos down on my bike—he had bigger mountains to climb. Nevertheless, each Sunday, I rode to the parking lot between our houses and waited for a minute, just in case. But when I rode off on his bike, one thing was certain:

I wasn't alone.

18 |

PRAYERS & WEED

Carlos did not want to be prayed for. A lifelong man of science, he did not believe in a deity. Fate was a load of bullshit. Divine intervention? Not a thing.

So he couldn't understand why people kept saying it to him. "I'm praying for you," they'd intone, gently and reverently placing their hands on his shoulders. "If God brings you to it, He will bring you through it."

That phrase usually sent him flying. "Keep your God," he would snap. "I've got something better: an arrogant oncologist."

If they weren't offering up prayers, chances were good they wanted to share their weed. Suddenly, everyone wanted to conncct Carlos with a source for medical marijuana: students, colleagues, neighbors. Even fellow triathletes got in on the action, handing off a piece of paper at races with the name and phone number of "their guy."

Everyone, it seemed, had "a guy," be it God or a guy with a dime bag.

"It's nice that people want to help," Carlos said one day, "but I don't need prayers and weed."

"I think people just want to feel like they're doing something," I surmised. I could certainly attest to the feeling. If I could have cured Carlos of cancer, I would have done it in a heartbeat. If I'd held the secret to taking away his pain, I would have done it. But unfortunately I was neither a superhero nor an arrogant oncologist. I was just me, and when it came to cancer, I didn't have much to offer. It was a terrible, powerless feeling. I could understand how offering prayers or weed could at least make someone feel as if they were doing something to help.

"You want to know what would really help?" Carlos said. I nodded. "I could really use some hard candy." His medication regimen had left him with a severely dry mouth. Drinking too much water nauseated him, but hard candy—specifically, mints or lemon drops—brought temporary relief.

After that day, I never left the house without a bag of candy in my purse. I was "that guy" for his Certs fix.

Supplication was difficult for Carlos, who was used to being self-reliant. He had no problem telling others to ask for help when they needed it, but he never considered taking that advice for himself. When those around asked with a pitying look how he was doing, when they made suggestions for treatment or offered prayers and weed, he eventually learned to state what he really needed: to shift the perspective from *Look how sick you are* to *Look how you're kicking cancer in the taint!* If you had a lemon drop, he wouldn't turn that down, either.

So that was exactly what we did. As triathletes, we were proficient in the language of pep talks. If Carlos needed a cheering squad, that was what he would get.

We took him out for coffee whenever he was feeling well; when he wasn't, we'd take pictures of our coffee and post them on his Facebook wall with random updates about our day, just as we would have talked about in person. The night before he was to undergo resection surgery to remove the diseased half of his liver, we flooded his phone with photos of his friends and family holding up signs of encouragement, just as we would in a race. When he was feeling particularly low, the Phoenix triathlon community collaborated to create a special music video to "Eye of the Tiger." Watching Speedo-clad triathletes dancing awkwardly made Carlos laugh so hard, it caused a nosebleed.

When he enrolled in an experimental treatment that required two weeks of total isolation in a hospital room, we set up shifts to keep him company through video chat. We ran in our tighty-whities in an Arizona knockoff of the Kona Underpants Run to raise money for a scholarship fund benefiting students at his college.

There were times when Carlos would shake his head, blushing with embarrassment, and call us ridiculous. But he relished the ridiculousness, too. We could tell.

We couldn't fix him—that was a job we had to leave up to the doctors. But the role we had was just as important. We could take his mind off things. We could bring him a sense of normalcy. We could buy him coffee and let him rifle through the pockets of our purses and backpacks, where he knew he could always find a peppermint. We danced in our Speedos. We made him laugh.

On his 50th birthday, we packed into his house for the biggest surprise of his life. The doctors hadn't thought he'd make it to this milestone, so we would be damned if we didn't celebrate.

"Modern medicine is amazing," Carlos said as he looked around the house in awe. "But you guys? You're my secret weapon."

19 |

YOU WILL DO THIS

For the six months leading up to Ironman Arizona, Carlos was too sick to train, much less race, but he retained his role as my coach and number-one fan.

The day before the race, Carlos asked a mutual friend of ours to tape a letter on my bike frame when I wasn't looking. I discovered it as I was setting up my gear in the early-morning hours before the race.

> You will do this. Say it to yourself a thousand times.
>
> Remember that during the race, just like during the several months of training you have endured, your body will question your sanity and give you hundreds of reasons to quit. Prepare your mind to have an answer for every question your body asks. Never forget why you are doing this.

Eat often. Pace yourself. And for fuck's sake, don't be a dumbass. Do those three things, and you will cross that finish line.

But regardless of the outcome of this one race, you have made me so proud. In my mind, you have always been, and always will be, an Ironman.

Carlos

Little did I know just how much I would need those words of encouragement to carry me through that day.

20 |

INTO THE LIGHT

In the months that pass between logging base miles to showing up at the start line on race day, endurance athletes endeavor to work out the kinks that may sabotage the race. We experiment with nutrition, shoes, clothes, and gear. We study elevation profiles and course maps with more focus than we ever studied anything in college. Because you reap what you sow when it comes to race day.

But sometimes, despite your very best efforts and intentions, you get kicked in the gut.

Ironman Arizona was my kick in the gut—literally.

In the 365 days that had passed since registering for Ironman Arizona with Carlos, I did everything I needed to ensure a perfect day—I trained well, ate right, and for the first time in my life experienced a complete absence of nerves about race day. I was confident. I was surrounded by friends.

I had a purpose and a plan. I could feel it in my bones: This was going to be the race of my life.

As I jumped into the water and splashed my way to the start line with 3,000 of my new best friends, I smiled and cheered. The sun was shining, the lake was warm, and my fellow athletes were surprisingly courteous in the crowded swim. Everything was perfect.

Until it wasn't.

Halfway through the 2.4-mile swim, I caught up to the blood-sport crowd. Punches were thrown, legs were grabbed, and I sustained a fierce kick to the ribs. Searing hot pain shot through me.

Normally, I'd unleash the kraken on anyone who dared to get physical with me, but I was too busy coughing up the gallons of bacteria-laden lake slime the kick had forced into my respiratory system. And anyway, this was Ironman, where the swim has often (and quite accurately) been compared to flailing around in a giant washing machine. Anything goes. So instead of complaining, I struggled and spat, finished the swim, and hopped on my bike for a 112-mile ride, putting the swim behind me. Everything was perfect again.

Until it wasn't.

Ten miles into the ride, I began to experience sharp pains in my side. Thinking they were stitches, I tried breathing exercises to stretch out my diaphragm. That only made things worse. Still, I soldiered on, with no intention of being derailed by a silly cramp. This was going to be the race of my life, dammit!

The next 102 miles can only be described as a shitshow. I vomited. I bonked. I ached and struggled to breathe. My speed on the bike devolved as the miles passed, and I reached transition surprised that I was still upright. I was in more pain than I had ever experienced before.

But I still had 26.2 miles of running to do. As I leaned over to lace up my shoes, the pain in my side was excruciating. But I stubbornly mustered up a smile. I was going to run. Period. Everything was going to be perfect again.

Until it wasn't.

It's been said that the Ironman marathon is the place where you meet yourself—inner voices that never existed before suddenly roar, weaknesses neglected in training become painfully clear, and new reserves of strength manifest themselves in awe-inspiring ways.

I met myself at mile 10. And let me tell you: I'm a real asshole.

Things I would never even *think* to say to another human being, much less one in pain, became perfectly acceptable to say to myself. Horrible, vile things blared between my ears with every step:

How is this race honoring Carlos? You are an embarrassment.

You write for a running magazine, and you can't even hold a 13-minute mile? Pathetic.

Neil finished this in 10 hours, and he's waiting for you. I bet he's mortified to even admit you're his partner. You don't deserve him.

Your family flew all the way out here to cheer you on. You wasted their time.

Everyone's making fun of you. Rightfully so.

Just quit. You don't deserve to be called an Ironman.

As I ran along the crowd-lined sidewalk, I pulled my hat low over my eyebrows and tucked my chin, letting the darkness consume me. With every wretched thought, I felt my legs get heavier and heavier until I couldn't run anymore. In front of hundreds of people, I slowed to a walk, refusing to look up.

You loser.

Suddenly, I felt myself enveloped by one pair of arms and then another. I looked up in shock and realized my walk had begun near a large group of my friends. Surrounded by their warmth and support, I felt myself begin to cry.

Christine squeezed my shoulders. Ashly kissed me on the cheek and wiped away my tears. Dre put his arm around me and walked at my side. He passed me off to Jason, who held my hand as we broke into a jog. Heidi and Brian radiated quiet, calm strength. My family hugged me tight at mile 20. Neil told me he loved me and that he was proud. I smiled at a row of touching, funny signs Carlos had asked a friend to stake in the ground at mile 23.

With every mile, I moved away from that inner darkness. Fourteen hours and 13 minutes after the start cannon fired, I entered the bright lights of the finish chute.

I know I could get away with writing about "the race of my life." I could easily churn out a contrived, inspirational paragraph or three about how I did an Ironman with a broken rib. I could write about mental fortitude or some such badassery. I could spew clichéd generic wisdom, such as "Pain is only in your head" or "Never, ever, ever give up."

But all those things would be half truths and certainly would not tell the story of my Ironman Arizona. In fact, if I learned one thing during the race that day, it was that on my own, I'm actually *not* that strong; those voices in my head made damn sure I was aware of that fact.

But the thing is, I wasn't on my own.

Pain is temporary. Anger is temporary. Shitshows are temporary. Embarrassment, darkness, broken ribs: temporary, temporary, temporary. And that day, I almost let myself believe they were a permanent part of my identity.

Instead, I learned from my friends and family what is permanent: love, support, joy. Few words were spoken, but their actions were sufficient to drown out the terrible voices in my head. Because of them, I can do anything.

Even an Ironman with a broken rib.

"That was a very dumb thing you did," Carlos said as I showed him my X-ray after a visit to the doctor the next day.

I shrugged. "What was I supposed to do?"

"A broken rib?" Carlos scoffed. "You quit the race and go to the hospital, that's what you're supposed to do."

"Nah." I draped the finisher's medal around Carlos's neck and grinned. "I came here for a fucking challenge, and I got one."

21 |

YOUR MOUNTAIN IS WAITING

Carlos could never resist a mountain. It wasn't its aesthetic appeal—never once did I see him stop to take in the view from a lookout point—nor was it for the physiological benefits of riding or hiking up one. A self-proclaimed desert rat, he didn't really care for the cooler temperatures of higher elevation, and the thin air of altitude sometimes gave him a headache.

No, he said he liked the mountain because it was a challenge; something to conquer. It stood there, mocking him with its steadfastness and inciting fear with its sheer size. Mountains made him feel tiny, and he hated that. If a mound of earth rose somewhere on the horizon, no matter how large or small, Carlos would plot his way to the top of it, just to show that he could.

Carlos was notorious for recruiting unwitting friends and training partners to tackle the mountain. "I'm doing a fun hike this weekend," he'd e-mail. "You should come along." These "fun" hikes usually yielded seizing quads and sunburned shoulders for everyone but Carlos, who whistled his way through the switchbacks. At least someone was having fun.

Every summer, he'd lure friends to long training weekends in high-altitude communities with promises of cooler weather and focused training, only to book the hotel rooms or campsites at the base of a mountain. To get to the top (and all its benefits), you had to ride your bike.

One mountain in particular held his fascination: Pico de Orizaba, the highest mountain in his native Mexico and the third-highest mountain in North America. He first saw it as a child on vacation and swore he'd climb it someday. There were other, more prestigious mountains—Everest or Kilimanjaro—but Pico de Orizaba, the first mountain he had ever seen, was seared into his brain.

Every now and then, at the summit of a particularly precipitous hike or bike ride, he'd bring up Pico de Orizaba and dream up plans for a big group of us to train together, travel to Mexico, and finally conquer the mountain.

It always came up in the context of "someday"—as in "Someday, when I retire from teaching" or "Someday, when I'm done with triathlon."

But when you're told you're going to die, "someday" no longer exists in your vocabulary. There's only today, and even that could be taken away from you at any time.

When Carlos was first diagnosed with cancer, he rolled his eyes when people asked about his bucket list. "I'm going to be around for a long time," he would scoff, waving his hand in dismissal. He simply wasn't worried about what he thought of as a clichéd desperate grab for life experiences.

But as the cancer progressed, it became clear that he had reason to worry. The scars from his surgeries hardened, limiting his range of motion. Chemotherapy treatments killed off nerve endings in his feet, creating a constant sensation of pins and needles when he walked. Lung tumors occupied the space where oxygen should go. A case of the sniffles became pneumonia, which became sepsis and kidney damage. His physicality suddenly had an expiration date.

"Fuck it," started the e-mail he sent to his friends one day. "I'm going to do it." Attached was an itinerary of his training and logistical plans for a Pico de Orizaba summit.

He didn't have to trick anyone into training with him this time. We were all in. The hikes that had once made us whine and moan with disdain became a nonnegotiable part of our weekends—up the mountains in Flagstaff, over the peaks of Tucson, to the bottom of the Grand Canyon and back up again. We said it was an act of kinship, but in actuality, it was a measure of caution—the doctors had advised Carlos against strenuous exercise of any sort. But Carlos, who was used to self-inflicted suffering with triathlon training, didn't believe there was anything strenuous about going for a walk. Which was what he called his excursions up the mountain—a walk.

These were really hard walks. The air was thin at high altitude, and often cold. There were steep grades and unsteady terrain. For even the healthiest of us, going for "a walk" was an ass kicker of a day. But for Carlos, whose lung capacity was shrinking by the day, it was a true test of body and mind.

Training was a group effort, but when it came time to depart for Mexico, Carlos set out alone. Though he had always imagined making the sojourn with friends and family, something changed in him while he was training. Pico de Orizaba was *his* mountain, and he needed to conquer it alone.

From his acclimatization hut at Piedra Grande, Carlos sent a brief update: Things were going as well as could reasonably be expected. A radiation treatment the week before had left him with a small, nagging cough, but he was otherwise fine. Some people expressed concern that the small cough would eventually turn into a big problem. Was he sure this was a smart idea? Perhaps he should wait until his lungs healed from the radiation treatment. Even through e-mail, we could hear Carlos scoff with incredulity.

"The mountain is here today," he wrote, "and so am I."

On the day of his planned summit, a group of us gathered to await an update. As we sat on couches, sipping coffee and waiting for word from Pico de Orizaba, the conversation turned to bucket lists. While training for his climb, Carlos had finally found a "someday" for a few other dreams, too: a hike up Yosemite's Half Dome, a tattoo on his upper arm, finding long-term security for a college scholarship fund he had established.

After wrapping up a lecture one day, he overheard several of his students talking about wanting to go skydiving someday. Carlos had never really considered skydiving before, but hearing his students say "someday" struck a nerve.

"Let's do it," he interjected.

"Right now?" they replied nervously.

"Yeah, sure," he said, opening his laptop to search for nearby tandem jumps. "Class trip, everyone!"

Later that week, a dozen engineering students and their favorite professor jumped out of a plane.

As we sat on the couch, awaiting word of Carlos's summit and laughing about our friend's fearlessness, I couldn't help but feel inadequate. That morning, I had spent two hours procrastinating on Facebook, hoping that cat memes and celebrity gossip would make my scheduled workout of hill repeats go away. Here I was, the possessor of a healthy body that still warranted the use of "someday" in my vocabulary, and I was bitching about hill repeats. What would I do if I knew I'd have no more somedays? More importantly, why wasn't I doing those things? Where was my mountain?

I thought about my bucket list of wants. I wanted to travel the world. I wanted to write a book. I wanted to take Neil to a cheesy wedding chapel in Vegas and upgrade him from insanely hot boyfriend to insanely hot husband. I wanted to hike to the top of a volcano and see the lava bubble and churn. I wanted to finally finish an open-water swim without freaking about lake zombies.

A laptop chimed, snapping me out of contemplation.

"You guys, you guys, you guys! It's him!" someone yelled excitedly. We gathered around the tiny screen of the computer as she clicked on the e-mail, inciting loud applause and whoops. There stood Carlos, tall and proud in his bright orange jacket. A balaclava covered most of his face, but the exposed wrinkles around his eyes left no doubt that he was smiling broadly under the layers of fleece.

Carlos had conquered that mountain—just because he could.

22 |

WHAT HURTS THE MOST

My friendship with Carlos was built on the shared pursuit of pain—riding bikes up mountain grinds, "easy" swims that always turned into breakneck competitions, pushing each other out of the way as we sprinted back to a trailhead ("Last one to the car has to pay for coffee!").

I thought I knew what pain was.

But when cancer consumed Carlos's body, "pain" took on a new meaning. Before, pain was part of a game we played, the result of a search for what we were made of. After his diagnosis, Carlos's body preemptively answered that question, and the answer was "those fucking tumors." I couldn't relate to the pain he was feeling the way I could empathize with a muscle cramp or a bike crash. I would have given anything for the days when our biggest problem was a muscle cramp or a bike crash.

There was nothing "fun" about this pain. Chemotherapy caused Carlos to curl into a fetal position on the floor for entire days and nights, surgeries left him covered in scars, experimental treatments tested his physical and mental limits. And yet somehow he remained willing, even grateful, to accept the pain. To him, the pain of Ironman and the pain of cancer were two sides of the same coin.

"The pain lets me know I'm alive," he said with determination. "When the pain stops, that means I've stopped."

Shortly after Carlos summited Pico de Orizaba, the tumors spread dramatically. The cancer had mutated to resist chemotherapy, and scans of his liver and lungs were riddled with abnormalities.

going to tell u something, Carlos texted late one night. promise you won't freak out.

Nothing freaks me out, sir, I replied. What's up?

at st. joe's. headaches, slurred speech. tumors in brain. surgery in a.m. to remove.

WHAT?!?

i know, he replied. catholic hospital, right?

The brain surgery, though successful, was merely a stopgap. Within weeks, the tumors returned, and so did the pain. The masses in his lungs continued to sprout, causing shortness of breath, and Carlos experienced daily debilitating headaches from the swelling in his brain. He arranged for other professors to teach his classes, as he found it hard to leave his house most days. On the rare symptom-free day, he still chose the comforts of home. It was just too exhausting to leave.

"It's time to talk about hospice care," the doctors said. "We can't try to cure you anymore, but we can manage your pain and keep you comfortable until the end."

"I don't *want* to be comfortable," Carlos huffed, pushing away the hospice brochures. "I'm not ready for that." To him, hospice meant giving up; it was where people went to die. Once he allowed palliative care, the pain would stop—but so would he.

But the question was no longer whether he would die but when. We steeled ourselves for the inevitable, hugging each other a little tighter with every "See you later," just in case it was the last time. I was scared—what kind of pain lay in wait for my friend? Was he really so stubborn that he would suffer until the end? I didn't know if I could bear the pain of watching that.

I was out for a run one autumn day when I got a text message from his daughter, Emily. The brain swelling had become too much to bear, and Carlos was being admitted to a hospice facility immediately. Ready or not, he had reached the beginning of the end. Heart in my throat, I rushed to the facility, preparing for a grim, somber scene.

Instead, I saw Carlos sitting up in bed, eating a burrito.

"Heyyyyy," he slurred with a groggy smile, "you're just in time for breakfast!"

Here's the thing about hospice: It's a place where people go to die, yes, but it's also a place where pain is removed. It's a place where cries of agony can be replaced with sighs of relief. It's a place where caregivers no longer have to shoulder the burden of sustaining life and instead can focus on simply loving the patient. It's a place where volunteers work tirelessly to make sure a dying guy can get almost anything he damn well pleases, including opiates and a breakfast burrito.

"Good drugs?" I asked as I leaned in to kiss his cheek. He gazed up at me through glazed eyes.

"Ohh, yeah," he purred. He stared over my shoulder for a second with an odd expression and then gestured for me to come closer, as if to tell me a secret.

"I can make myself see red flowers," he disclosed with glee. He squeezed his eyes tightly shut, then opened them rapidly, staring off into space with openmouthed awe. "Look! Look! Isn't that great?"

It's amazing what opiates and a good breakfast burrito can do.

Carlos was dying—that was an inescapable fact. But as difficult as it was for him to cede the battle, acceptance finally brought the warrior some relief. The fight, which was exhausting, was over. And for the first time since his diagnosis four years earlier, he looked calm. Peaceful, even. Seeing him at peace made me feel at peace, too.

For the next few days, I joined a rotation of friends and family members keeping vigil at his bedside, holding his hand as he moved in and out of sleep. Sometimes he'd stir and start a brief but surprisingly lucid conversation about riding bikes or current events. Other times he'd ask me to pluck a red flower from his field of vision. Then he'd fall asleep again, only to wake up confused and muttering.

"Where am I?"

"You're at hospice, sir."

"Why am I here?"

"Your nurse thought you'd be more comfortable here."

"Oh." He closed his eyes again, only to open one a few seconds later and whisper curiously, "Am I comfortable?"

"Yes." I smiled through tears. "Very."

Carlos squeezed my hand as he closed his eyes once more. "Good."

23 |

HE'S GONE

I was on the train when I got the text from Diane:

It's probably going to be soon. All the kids are with us. We're okay. Will keep you posted.

My train lurched to the right as it took a wide corner. The morning commuters scrambled to grab handles or chase down rolling coffee mugs. A gaggle of college students laughed loudly at a video playing on someone's phone screen. The man next to me rocked his head in time with the music blaring through his headphones. I sat at the back of the train, staring at the words on my phone screen:

It's probably going to be soon.

Shortly before Carlos took his final turn for the worse, Neil—now my husband—had been offered a job in Salt Lake City. It was an incredible opportunity for us to live and work in the town where he'd spent his childhood. But the timing of the move was horrible, Neil told his company—would it be possible to wait until I had finished supporting a friend through the end of his life? The answer from his higher-ups was no. A gentle, kind no, but a no nonetheless.

"Oh, for fuck's sake, Lacke." Carlos sighed with irritation when I nervously relayed the news. "Why would you even ask his company that?"

"Well, I thought I should be here for—"

"What, sit around and wait for me to die?" he scoffed. "Come on, don't be a dumbass. This is a good opportunity that will last longer than I will. Go."

With a truckload of guilt and apprehension, I moved to Salt Lake City. I flew back to Phoenix often to check on Carlos, grateful for the stockpile of frequent flier miles I had accrued on my credit card from years of triathlon expenditures. Finally, this sport had paid me back.

In my naïveté, I had assumed that I would be able to make it back to Phoenix when the time came for him to die. I would drop everything, get on the next flight, and rush to his bedside, as I had so many times before. But now, on the Salt Lake City Red Line, it was clear that that wasn't going to happen.

I didn't know what to do. Despite the sad news, I didn't feel like crying. My default setting was to spring into action—*Stop this train! I want to get off!*—but to do what? Teleport to Phoenix? Stop Carlos from dying? Anything I could do would be completely useless. I bowed my head and closed my eyes, clasping my hands so tightly my knuckles turned white.

I don't know why I prayed on the train, honestly. Like Carlos, I'm not much of a God person. I believe things happen because people make them happen, not some white-bearded-flowing-robed creature in the sky. Even the act of praying for Carlos made me wonder if he could somehow hear it, and if he could, was he rolling his eyes at me?

But I did it anyway. I prayed that Carlos wouldn't feel any pain. I prayed for him to be free of fear. I prayed for his family to be strong. I prayed that he knew just how much he was loved.

The train bell clanged as it came to my stop, a platform in front of the local university. I looked up at the row of buildings outside my window. In 15 minutes, I had an interview for a very promising teaching job on campus. I looked at the message on my phone once more and wondered if I should cancel.

Oh, for fuck's sake, Lacke. What else are you going to do? Sit around and wait for me to die?

"Hold the door!" I called out as I gathered my portfolio and coat to rush off the train. Before entering my interview, I took a deep breath, closed my eyes, and thought of Carlos. The image I conjured up wasn't one of him lying in bed, dying; instead, he was reclining behind his desk on campus, smiling and catching flying M&M's in his mouth.

I don't remember much about that interview except that I was offered the job on the spot. While waiting for a human resources person to arrive with the obligatory new-hire forms, I excused myself and sneaked into the hallway to peek at my phone. A message from Emily was waiting:

He's gone.

24 |

ABOVE ALL

Carlos left behind very few instructions for his funeral. He had insisted that it didn't matter to him, because funerals were for the living, and he wouldn't be there.

The funeral homes in Phoenix were all too small to host an event honoring Carlos Nunez. Instead, hundreds of us packed into an event center on a Sunday morning: students and faculty members, neighbors, friends, and what seemed like every triathlete in the tri-state area. A few had even flown in from Europe. After meeting Carlos at overseas Ironman races, they'd maintained friendships spanning many years and many more miles.

The gang from Ironman St. George was there, and we all laughed as we recounted how he had done the race with a broken bike.

The very nice boy Carlos had tried to set me up with years ago was there, as was his new wife, who is a lovely person—and, in a cheeky twist, has an Ironman PR faster than anything Carlos ever recorded.

His oncology team was there, including Stern Nurse, who (finally) admitted that Carlos had been her favorite patient.

A former student announced that he had signed up to do his very first Ironman and would use the race to raise money for the Carlos Nunez scholarship fund.

We laughed and cried, but mostly we laughed. Despite his assertion to the contrary, Carlos Nunez was definitely there with us that day.

And, as I had promised four years earlier in that hotel room in Flagstaff, I wrote a eulogy for my best friend.

"How are you?"

When Carlos Nunez asked that question, he wasn't engaging in social niceties. He truly wanted to know the answer.

Each of us knew Carlos in different ways—accomplished professor, 13-time Ironman, champion for social justice, congenial neighbor, devoted family man. In all those roles, his trademark was the same: Carlos would ask, "How are you?" and he'd drop everything to hear the answer. For you, he had all the time in the world.

We've learned many lessons from Carlos during his 50 years on earth: Show up. Work hard. Learn from your mistakes. Stand up for what you believe in. Expect better. Fight. And above all, be good to others.

Carlos Nunez lives on in us all. When you leave today, you are not leaving Carlos behind—you are carrying him into the world. His legacy shines every time you go out of your way to make someone's day a little better, when you treat strangers like you would a friend, when you offer help even when you don't have the time. Carlos lives on in the smile that comes after you stop to ask "How are you?"—and mean it.

25 |

THE NEW NORMAL

"You know you'll spend more on fixing up this bike than what it's worth, right?"

My bike mechanic smiled—not kindly but in that *you-poor-sap-how-can-you-be-so-stupid?* kind of way.

I could have done without the attitude, but he was right. Ten years ago, when Carlos's tri bike was a brand-new specimen, it was considered top of the line. The technology was state of the art, the frame geometry innovative, the brand coveted. But that was 10 years ago. In comparison to the other bikes in my garage, this one was an outdated piece of shit. Correction: an outdated piece of shit about to cost me a lot of money.

The tires were empty and cracked, the skewers were missing, and the frame was covered in dust. A twisted cobweb dangled from the handlebars, which dangled from the frame by the shifter cables.

"You really want to ride this?" the bike mechanic asked. I nodded.

He cocked his head curiously. "Don't you have other bikes?"

I nodded again. "But I want to ride *this* bike."

He sighed, muttered something under his breath (*you-poor-sap-how-can-you-be-so-stupid?*), and began writing up a repair estimate.

Technically, this outdated piece of shit did not belong to me. Carlos had insisted that I hang on to it after I finished Ironman Arizona, despite my serious doubts that I'd ever do another Ironman.

"I'm sure someone else can use it now," I said to him after the race. "What about your neighbor? Didn't you say he wanted to do a triathlon?"

Carlos took a sip of his coffee and considered the proposal. Then he shook his head. "Nah. I want you to hang on to it for a while longer. You're not done with it yet."

Every now and then, he'd inquire about the bike. I'd say it was doing fine.

"You're keeping her clean?"

"Yes, sir."

"Don't break the fucking bike."

"I'm trying not to."

"It's a very nice bike, you know."

"I know."

What I didn't tell him was that I hadn't ridden that bike since Ironman Arizona. Along with the loss of our regular Sunday-morning rides had gone my motivation to train for triathlons. Long rides just weren't as much fun without him as a conversation partner.

Then Carlos died. And his bike sat in my garage, collecting dust.

The night before his funeral, my friend Ashly asked how I was holding up. "I haven't cried yet," I confessed. "Do you think that's weird?"

"People grieve in different ways, Susan," Ashly replied. "I don't think that's weird at all."

Still, I felt like I was doing the grief thing wrong—wasn't I supposed to be doing *something*? My closest friend was dead. Shouldn't I be wailing? Gnashing my teeth? Shaking my fists at the sky in anger? Surely if I could do those things, I could check off a few boxes in the grieving process and get my life back to normal. I tried many times to will a watershed moment into being; it never worked.

Grief is a weird journey. As it turns out, you can't really push through it to get to the finish line, because there isn't a finish line. Even the idea of getting back to "normal" is an absurd one. Months after the funeral, I'd still forget that Carlos wasn't alive anymore. Something would happen, and

I'd think, *Wait until Carlos hears about this.* Sometimes I'd even go so far as to pull out my phone to text him. And then I'd feel the sharp pang of reality.

I think Carlos knew I would have a difficult time adjusting to the new normal. Shortly before he died, we talked about what he wanted done with his ashes. One of the things he requested was that they be sprinkled in Austria, the site of his first Ironman. He asked if I'd do the race and take him along for the ride.

"It's perfect," he said excitedly. "You've already got my bike!"

Ah, yes. That outdated piece of shit in my garage. It had been three years since I'd last ridden it. Could it make it through another Ironman? Could *I* make it through another Ironman?

"Wait a second." I gave Carlos a suspicious look. "Is this why you had me keep your bike?"

"I don't know what you're talking about, Susan," Carlos scoffed, looking down at his coffee cup in an unsuccessful attempt to hide a mischievous grin.

Three months after Carlos died, I set out to make good on my promise. I cleared the cobwebs and lifted the bike off the rack it had languished on for far too long. Part of me felt guilty for neglecting the only tangible token I had of my best friend; the other part of me was resentful. Did I really have to ride this outdated piece of shit? For an Ironman, no less?

After picking up the spiffed-up bike from the mechanic, I took it out for a long ride in the sunshine.

This could be the heartwarming part of the story where I say that putting all my disposable income into fixing up this bike turned it into a brand-new steed, that this 10-year-old machine had suddenly been transformed into a sleek bolt of greased lightning.

Or maybe this could be the cathartic part of the story where I say that riding my best friend's bike was an intense moment and that at the summit of some beautiful mountain, I finally cried.

But neither of those things happened. I did not cry, and the outdated piece of shit was still an outdated piece of shit.

And yet on that ride, I felt better. Lighter. Almost—dare I say?—normal. *Wait until Carlos hears about this,* I thought.

Well, almost normal. The new normal, I supposed.

I looked down at the bike and smiled.

"It's been a while," I said. "We've got a lot to talk about."

26 |

THERE'S A BIKE IN THOSE TREES

Sometimes there is the Plan. And then there is What Actually Happens.

The plan: I fly to Austria and do the Ironman. After the race is over, I identify a place to scatter Carlos's ashes. A simple and poignant tribute.

What actually happened: Not that.

The days leading up to the race were equal parts bizarre and emotional. Weeks after picking up a portion of Carlos's ashes from his family, I still hadn't figured out how I was going to actually race with his remains. Diane gave me a small amount—no bigger than a deck of cards—in a satin lavender bag from the funeral home.

"You're going to make him so proud, Susan," Diane said as she handed me the satchel containing part of my best friend. My mind rushed with a million thoughts: *Is it rude to put him in my purse? What parts of his body are in this bag? Does he know he's in my purse right now? Should I open the pocket so it's not so dark in there?*

But the biggest question: *How the hell am I supposed to race with this little purple sack?*

Later that week, I went to the sporting goods store, Carlos still tucked in a pocket of my purse.

"Can I help you?" the clerk asked.

"Sure," I said. "I'm looking for some kind of small dry bag. Maybe one I can wear around my neck?"

"We've got a few options," he said, leading me to the water-sports aisle. "What activity are you doing, and what do you need to keep dry?"

"An Ironman triathlon," I replied, "and, uh, some human remains."

The clerk's expression quickly changed from cheerful to disturbed. "I'm sorry, what did you—"

"An iPhone!" I quickly interrupted, laughing nervously at the realization of just how deranged I sounded. "I need to keep an iPhone dry!"

The clerk raised an eyebrow and pointed at a row of dry bags on display. "You'll probably find what you need here."

He turned on his heel and sped away, most likely in search of a security guard.

Neil and I flew to Austria, Carlos in tow. As the plane descended over the pristine lakes and lush green forests of the Austrian Alps, my heart fluttered. I couldn't wait to race.

But another problem quickly revealed itself—Carlos's bike hadn't made the trip. When we landed at our destination, the bike box was conspicuously absent from the parade of suitcases unloaded at the baggage claim.

"I think it might be in Paris," the apathetic airline agent said as he typed a series of commands into his computer.

"You *think*?" I asked, feeling my heartbeat pound in my ears. This couldn't be happening.

"We will try to confirm," he replied without the least bit of interest. "If we find it, we'll get it to you right away."

"If you find it?" I screeched. "*If*? I flew here with a bike. I need a bike! I have a race in two days!" I was every cliché of a demanding, entitled American, and the Austrian agent was having none of it. His voice and demeanor remained monotone: "I'll see what I can do."

For the next 24 hours, the updates from the airline were scattershot and devoid of hope: *The bike has been located in Paris—It seems it is in Frankfurt now—We think it might have been delivered to our lost-luggage storage in Berlin—We can't find it. Are you certain you brought it?*

My panic increased with every phone call. I tossed and turned, unable to sleep. Without a bike, I wouldn't be able to follow through on the promise I'd made to Carlos.

Mere hours before the race, a bike box appeared in the doorway of my hotel room. I barely recognized the case: Its hard shell was cracked in two places, the handles were missing, and a wheel had come loose from its socket. Somewhere in Paris/Frankfurt/Berlin/God-Knows-Where, this case had been drop-kicked from a cargo hold.

I held my breath as I opened the broken latches. Neil inspected the contents, nodding with a relieved sigh. The bike, by some miracle, had emerged from its impromptu transnational tour unscathed.

Carlos had made it to Austria. So had his bike. I could finally race. I put on my swim cap, tucked the dry bag containing Carlos's ashes into my wetsuit, kissed my husband, and headed to the start line. It was time for one last Ironman.

***

Fifteen minutes before the race, someone hugged me. With a heavy European accent, a tall, bearded man told me he loved me and was proud of me. *You vill do zis, ja!*

"Who was that?" Neil asked as my cheerleader walked off.

"I have no idea," I said, laughing and dumbfounded. God, I loved Ironman starts. I recalled seeing my first start in Coeur d'Alene, standing there awkwardly, watching for

Carlos, amid the buzz, the excitement, the hugs and high fives. So much had changed since that race, yet I still got goose bumps at every start line.

Carlos was with me today—literally. He was hanging out in a tiny waterproof pouch around my neck while I swam in the crisp waters of the Austrian lake. He was right next to my heart as I rolled out on his bike for the challenging bike ride. His voice was in my head—*Eat. Pace yourself. Don't be a dumbass.* This was not my race. This was Carlos's. I was just the vehicle.

He was definitely there at mile 20, when I dropped my chain on the first climb: *Just fix it and get back on.* And he was there at mile 25, when I couldn't find the right gear to shift into: *Just ride the damn bike like I taught you to.* He was there at mile 30, when I began having trouble shifting from my big ring to my small ring. I left it in the hardest gear, gritted my teeth, and pushed the pedals. *Ironman is supposed to be hard.* The corner of the bag containing his remains jabbed at my chest. At this point, Carlos was starting to chafe both my psyche and my skin.

At the base of the course's biggest climb, a steep monster known as Rupertiberg, the bike simply refused to shift. I put my head down and grunted. *It's supposed to be hard*, I repeated to myself. My legs burned. My vision blurred. I cursed the outdated piece of shit I was riding. I cursed Carlos. This was all his fault.

I could barely breathe as I crested the climb, standing up on the pedals for leverage. Between my feet, I felt a loud, sudden clatter. The wheels suddenly stopped, sending me flying onto the pavement.

What the hell, Lacke?

I sat up gingerly and turned my attention to the mangled bike beside me. The derailleur, which was supposed to be affixed to the frame, was dangling from the chain. The attachment must have come loose during the jostling of travel; the race had dislodged the bolt completely. The bike was unridable.

"Fuck!" I screamed, slamming my fist on the pavement in frustration. This couldn't be happening. My breaths became shorter and shallower as I sat on the side of the road, watching fellow racers whiz by on the course. A few asked if I was okay. One, thinking I had a flat tire, tossed a spare tube my way.

For some reason, it was that tube that did me in. Not the broken bike, not my tired legs, not the plastic bag poking a hole in my rib cage—it was the realization that I couldn't muscle my way out of this bad situation. I had been outstubborned. The levee broke, and the tears finally came.

I cried because Carlos had never quit a race, and I was about to fail him. I cried because he would have found a way to jerry-rig that broken bike, get to transition, and run to the finish line. I cried because I was such a dumbass. I cried because I couldn't tell him about this over a cup of coffee when I got home. I cried because I had a dead man hanging in a bag around my neck. I cried because I missed him.

All I could do was hyperventilate on the side of the road, clutching the bag of ashes in my hand. "I'm so sorry, Carlos. I'm so sorry."

"Are you okay?" a rider asked as he slowed to approach me. Was I? I didn't know, but I nodded, waving him away. I couldn't face that question anymore. I shifted my weight and swung my legs over the guardrail on the side of the road, turning my back to the events behind me.

I inhaled sharply. "Holy shit!"

That view. For the entirety of my meltdown, I had never once bothered to look up. But from here, the highest point of the course, the views were absolutely stunning. There were majestic mountains and sparkling lakes. Far below, tucked among lush green hills, was a small village, its quaint cathedral poking out from a grove of trees.

I understood why Carlos had picked this place for me to visit. It was magical—one of the most beautiful, tranquil scenes I had ever encountered. In my mind, I could see him doing his first Ironman here, climbing this hill, taking in this view, and feeling so alive.

It's not about the Ironman. It was never about the Ironman.

"Hey, you okay?" Someone tapped me on the shoulder. It was a race official, conducting a sweep of the course for riders who were unable to finish the race.

"Yeah, I'm okay," I said, wiping away the last of my tears. And I meant it.

***

Neil, who was also racing that day, was surprised to see me waiting at the finish line when he crossed. "What happened?" he asked. I broke down again as I recounted my shitshow of a day—the dropped chain, the missing bolt, the crash.

He pulled me in for a hug. "You know what this means, right?" I didn't. Neil poked the lump protruding under my shirt. "That's the place Carlos wanted you to scatter his ashes."

I had been so focused on finishing the race that I hadn't even thought about scattering the ashes. Had Carlos really been trying to send me a message? Did he really have to go to all that trouble just to get me to look up? Neil laughed and kissed my forehead: "You're hardheaded, babe. He knew that."

***

The plan: I fly to Austria and do the Ironman. Afterward, I figure out where to scatter Carlos's ashes.

What actually happened: Carlos led me to the place during the race.

Early that evening, I drove back up to the top of the mountain and looked out at the view once more. In the twilight, the setting was even more idyllic than before.

With a deep breath, I opened the satin bag. "Thank you, sir," I whispered. "I love you very much."

I watched his ashes float down into the ravine below, dusting the leaves of the trees. It was exactly where he wanted to be.

"By the way," I smiled mischievously, "I think you'll need this."

And then I threw that damned bike off the bridge, too. It flew gracefully through the air, then landed on the ash-dusted forest canopy. A random bike in a random tree. To a passerby, it wouldn't make a bit of sense. It was the perfect metaphor for our friendship.

I think it would have made Carlos laugh.

God knows I did.

AUTHOR'S NOTE

All the events in this book are true; however, the stories are pieced together from the archives of e-mails, text messages, my column in *Competitor* magazine, diary entries, and my own memory. The latter two are colored by my own perspective and the more-than-occasional bottle (fine, *box*) of wine. Were Carlos here today, he might tell some stories differently—particularly a version of events in which he is less a callous asshole and I am even more an incompetent dolt. Also, he would make sure the words "ruggedly handsome" appeared in the vicinity of his name at least seven times in this book.

Let that be a warning to all my friends and family—don't die before me, or I might write a book calling you a callous asshole.

This is one story. It has a lot of unique factors. It is not intended to be representative of all triathletes, of all people with cancer, or of all friendships. This is not a how-to manual about triathlon or cancer—there are plenty of experts on those topics. In matters of life, death, and Ironman, please listen to them.

Not every conversation I had with Carlos was a profound, life-changing experience. We had a lot of talks about stupid stuff like Sarah Palin or the right way to eat Double Stuf Oreos. I left out a lot of stories, like the time Carlos asked if I'd be willing to peek at his saddle sore to tell him if it looked infected (I was not willing).

I also left out several events in our history that Carlos specifically asked me not to write about. If you have a best friend, you understand Best Friend Privilege. Some secrets simply must stay secret.

It was no secret that I loved Carlos Nunez. I hope you, dear reader, are lucky enough to have a mentor like him.

ACKNOWLEDGMENTS

Diane, Claudia, Emily, and Andrew Nunez: I am in constant awe of your grace, love, and generosity. Thank you.

Casey Blaine, we did it. Holy shit, we did it! As a thank-you gift to you, I will impose a seven-day hiatus during which I will not e-mail you with dumb questions. (Okay, maybe only five.) (You know what? Maybe check your inbox tomorrow.)

Good editors can make chicken salad from chicken—well, you know what I mean. After their impeccable work on this book, Andy Read, Connie Oehring, and Sarah Gorecki will probably never eat chicken salad again.

Dave Trendler patiently listened to all my big marketing ideas for this book, then even more patiently demonstrated why I really should just stick to my day job. The guy is good.

Everything I know about writing, I learned from Matt Frazier, T.J. Murphy, Somyr McLean Perry, Mario Fraioli, Brian Metzler, Julia Polloreno, Jene Shaw, Liz Hichens, Mary Brown Malouf, and Glen Warchol.

Someone once told me that you should never be the smartest person in the room. If you are, you need to surround yourself with people who push you to do more and be better. Meghan Boyle, Colleen Junck, Dan Quick, Heidi and Brian Lueb, Ashly Wenzel, Jacob DeMik, Beth Gabavics, Jason and Karen Bahamundi, The Whales, and Team Triple Sports: I'm glad you're in my room. Please ignore the padlock on the door.

The Lackes raised me, the Boyles adopted me, and the Manvilles claimed me as their own. In the family lottery, I hit the jackpot three times.

Alex Manville has never been too cool to hang out with me, even though she is entirely too cool to hang out with me. XOXO, kiddo.

Neil Manville, you believed in me when I didn't believe in myself. You also ate the last piece of cheesecake in the fridge after I explicitly told you not to. "For better or for worse," indeed. I love you for it all.

ABOUT THE AUTHOR

Susan Lacke is a writer, professor, and endurance athlete whose work regularly appears in *Competitor, Triathlete, Women's Running,* and *Salt Lake* magazines. She lives in Salt Lake City, Utah, with four animals: a labrador, a cattle dog, a miniature pinscher, and a freakishly tall husband named Neil. Lacke claims to be of sound mind, though this has yet to be substantiated by a medical professional.